Pedagogy of Political Science

Pedagogy of Political Science

Pankaj Arora
Department of Education [CIE]
University of Delhi, Delhi

SHIPRA

₹ 750; US$ 37.50
ISBN: 978-93-86262-66-0

First Published in India in 2018

Pedagogy of Political Science

Published by:
SHIPRA PUBLICATIONS
LG 18-19, Pankaj Central Market
I.P. Ext., Patparganj, Delhi 110092, India
Tel.: +91 11 2223 5152/6152
E-mail: info@shiprapublication.com
www.shiprapublication.com

Dedicated to

My Students

Who supported and inspired me to bring this book

Contents

Foreword

Political Science as a discipline carries the very daunting responsibility of nurturing young students to become responsible, committed and critical citizens for the nation on the one hand and critical thinkers and theory builders on the other. The aims of teaching Political Science in schools include inculcation of secular and democratic attitudes and values as enshrined in the Indian Constitution and building commitment towards the economic and social development of the country.

In the present school curriculum, Political Science is taught as a compulsory subject to all students upto the secondary school level and as a specialized optional course at the senior secondary stage. The idea underlying this is that by the end of the secondary stage, every student should have an understanding of how political institutions and processes work. For those who choose to specialize in it at the senior secondary stage, the theoretical underpinnings of political thought and systems and an analytical perspective of problems like terrorism, marginalization, social discrimination, urban migration, etc. are the envisaged objectives. The success of this is dependent on the pedagogic stance that the teacher uses in the classroom. If the emphasis is on factual narration of the text, information may get shared but knowledge construction by the learner takes a backseat. On the other hand, a learner centric pedagogic stance which optimizes learner participation and visualizes his/her contribution as significant to the knowledge construction process ensures that real learning and perspective building take place. Achieving this is a very big challenge for teachers. Recognizing the gaps and challenges that exist, the present book has been designed as a rich resource for teachers to revitalize the teaching of Political Science by making it more relevant, animated and linked to the real issues that characterize the polity and society of a nation.

Dr. Pankaj Arora is passionate about the subject and in my association with him over the last 25 years, I have seen him igniting the flame among his students through the use of both scholastic and co-scholastic activities,

The contents of the book focus on different techniques, strategies and activities that lend themselves to effective teaching of Political Science. Embedded in them is also the concern for values like empathy, brotherhood, tolerance and respect for diversity. Issues of curriculum, evaluation and addressing diversity also find detailed discussion. The attempt is to equip teachers with new ideas and ways of transacting their classes so that knowledge construction is facilitated. Most of the suggested strategies perceive the learner to be a co-constructor of knowledge.

Other significant features of the book include a detailed description of the origin of the discipline of political science as a school subject and also carry contemporary perceptions of teachers and students. What is commendable is that the overall pedagogic stance takes cognizance of the nature of the learner, the context in which the learning takes place and the content that has to be learnt. It suggests ways in which they can be synchronized and exemplifies the same. It is thus hoped that both pre-service and in-service teachers will benefit from this book.

At the end, I would like to congratulate Dr. Pankaj Arora for this contribution and the vast terrain that it covers. It is said that learning occurs both overtly and covertly. A book like this indeed ensures that this happens. His rich insights, familiarity with the school system, deep concern for the more esoteric goals of Political Science and long innings as a teacher educator have helped to make this, 'a book with a difference!'

Professor Namita Ranganathan
Head & Dean
Central Institute of Education [CIE]
Faculty of Education
University of Delhi
Delhi 110007

Deepawali 2017

Preface

Teachers get life from their students. For a teacher it is important to take into account the needs of the learners, their socio-cultural background, their previous knowledge and experiences. It is extremely significant to take note the way students participate in the class, and how eager they are to learn new things and the vice versa. The expressions on the students' face during the course of the classroom processes can itself help a teacher to understand how effectively the class has been going on, how the methodology is able to engage the learners in the development of the lessons and what all changes are required to be incorporated so as to make it more appropriate. I firmly believe that the journey of learning is a never ending journey and we can learn something new from our changing environment, the changing trends and from each and every individual around us.

My students who come from different parts of the country, with diverse backgrounds, and diverging ideas and opinions, have always been my source of inspiration and also a guiding force who help me in realising the responsibilities of a Teacher Educator.

Political Science Pedagogy has always been my area of interest and also one of my specialisations. I have been experimenting with need and significance of lesson planning for 6 years and also with evaluation reports. The 100s of students with whom I got associated till now have helped me in realising the importance of establishing a link between Educational theory and the life experiences of the students.

Creating an active Civics Society since the year 1997, with a goal to make the teaching-learning process more interesting and lively by honing not just the understanding skills of the students but also their creative skills by involving them in debates, discussions, visit to parliament, film screening and so on helped me in maintaining my full faith in the power of 'learning by doing' and 'experimentation' for the teaching learning of Political Science and creating and maintaining a democratic classroom environment.

As Education and Democracy are very much interconnected so, in order to make the present and future citizens aware of the significance of the two, we are required to make our school and classroom environment more democratic. The classroom environment, the teacher's attitude, the Pedagogic processes and methods that they adopt, leaves a very strong message for the learners.

Effective teaching-learning takes place when the teacher takes into account the needs of all the learners and provides each and every learner with equal opportunities to take part in the classroom processes and activities. This helps in making the classroom environment democratic, where each and every student is given the freedom to have a voice in the classroom, teacher and students value democratic ideals of freedom, equality, caring, empathy, dignity, and the common good and learning goes beyond the four walls of the classroom.

With the assemblage of my understanding and reflections as a pedagogue, I thought of documenting my experiments in different methodologies of teaching this subject and compiling it in the form of a book on *Pedagogy of Political Science*. In order to compile this book, I found it to be quintessential to include the views and suggestions of Political Science in service school teachers, students and teacher educators. Their views on diverse themes related to methodology and the nature and scope of political science and about various pedagogic processes and issues were taken into account while compiling this book. Efforts were made to prepare a book which not only focuses on the Political Science pedagogy and the various teaching learning methods and approaches, but which is a holistic book with the main focus on teaching-learning and growth of the subject of Political Science in the Indian context and explaining the significant theories with practical examples.

This book, based on my experiences and experiments as a pedagogue of political science, encompasses chapters on varied themes ranging from the basic theoretical concepts such as the Origin and Growth of Social Science, Political Science as a discipline of knowledge, Interdisciplinary Nature of Political Science etc., and also analytical and critical concepts such as the Relationship of Political Science with other Social Science subjects, Teaching-Learning Approaches and Methods in Political Science, Political Science and Teacher Education, Growth of a Reflective Political Science Teacher, Critical pedagogy, Inclusive and Democratic Classroom for Political Science, evaluation in Political Science and so on.

I am thankful for the continuous motivation and support provided by the Present Head of the Department of Education, University of Delhi Professor Namita Ranganathan, who is my mentor, friend and a great human being.

I am also very thankful to Dr. Geeta Sahni who has been a very supportive colleague and has helped me in growing as a pedagogue since my initial years in CIE. Documenting my experiences and experiments would not have been possible without the active support of my M.Phil and Ph.D Scholar Ms Bhageshwari Sharma.

I am also thankful to my wife Smita who is also a Political science teacher and my daughter Rupal who is a Political Science Student. The discussions and debates revolving around the questions how Political Science should be taught taken place with them at different stages of writing this book have helped me in closely understanding a teachers' and a students' perspective.

Lastly, I want to express my thanks to the Research Council of University of Delhi for supporting me to conduct the research project which helped me to culminate it in the form of this Pedagogy book.

With a hope that this book will prove useful for the Students/ Scholars and Practitioners (Pre Service and In Service) in the field of research, teaching and learning of Political Science. Readers' valuable feedback will be of great help in bringing the next edition of this book.

Readers' valuable feedback will be of great help in bringing the next edition of this book.

Dr. Pankaj Arora
Associate Professor
Department of Education
University of Delhi
E-mail id: pankajcie@yahoo.com

24/10/2017
United Nations Day

1

Exploring the Science of Society

Human Society has become a complex entity, the more we try to understand it, the more complicated it becomes. In the present world, when human life has become a web of crisscross equations, starting from nowhere and reaching out to another web, it becomes even more complicated. Some 40-50 years ago, we used to define primary human needs as food, shelter and clothing, as the bare minimum necessities for all living creatures on this earth. Gradually, with the development of civic amenities and the use of Technology in our day-to-day life, instead of making life simple and straight-forward, we have further, complicated it.

Today, human life is multi-faceted, be it in the field of Social, Political, Economic, Psychological, Emotional, Scientific, Literature and so on. The question regarding the methods of understanding these dynamics of human life is a matter of concern. At all times of development, thinkers have tried their level best to comprehend this critical aspect about the study of human life. Another critical question that arises is where should we start to understand this web of human relations?

This web could, further, be referred to as Society. For a long period of time, thinkers who have tried defining society have got entrapped in an endless debate about the individual and society. The philosophers of ancient Greece namely, Socrates, Plato, and Aristotle, were the first in the series who reflected on human society, and they tried to project models in which society should operate. Thereafter, for centuries, Social and Political theorists along with the philosophers kept exploring answers to the same question. Many Romans also followed the same line of thought. For many centuries, analysis of society, largely remained philosophical. Thinkers did not attempt to understand society in a systematic manner. In other words, they lacked systematic analysis of this structure and the working of human relationships at the micro level of the family and the macro level of human society. Although, the Greek and Roman philosophers did construct grand models and schemes about the individuals and their equations, yet, they failed to look at the modus operandi of the workings of these Societies.

It's only in the modern world, that attempts to define human society were made on some systematic basis, post the industrial revolution. Human relationships were being looked at through a different perspective. It was at this time, that the social thinkers tried to understand Society through an economic perspective, dominating all other perspectives; or through the political perspective by belittling others. There were huge gaps in the interpretation of these different perspectives, with reference to the comprehensive understanding of Society. In other words, we can say that these different perspectives complemented each other, whereas, a few thinkers perceived them as parallel. This was the time when new structures of knowledge were taking shape, while on the other hand, the French revolution, American Freedom Movement, Imperialism and Colonialism helped the evolution of large Nation-States.

Social Science under the Influence of Natural Science

However, from the 18th century onwards, in Europe, important changes took place in the way of understanding of Society and the place of the individuals in it. Many significant inventions took place in the field of science to understand the composition of the physical world which surrounds human beings. This was the time when natural sciences were in their infancy and were trying to develop systematic methods for the study of the physical world and the role of individuals in it. The term 'social science' first appeared in 1824, as an inquiry into "principles of distribution of wealth." Natural Sciences were being increasingly recognized and valued for generating this new knowledge, which was called scientific. This growth of Natural Sciences gave birth to an enquiry, if such Scientific and Rational approaches can be applied to the relationships of humans in Society. The social thinkers of the 20th century were struggling to explore if human experiences and behaviors could be better understood with the help of these approaches of Natural Sciences.

The Industrial Revolution and the renaissance were contemporary to the Scientific and Technological development and laid the transformation for an urban, industrial and mechanized living style. Agriculture, methods of production, transportation and communication brought large scale changes in the life of human beings and a greater variety of occupations emerged. In the Open the Social Sciences, Gulbenkian Commission Report (1999) it has been mentioned that the impact of the natural sciences, both in academia and the larger society, catalyzed an attempt to introduce scientific methodologies in those disciplines that were concerned with humans and society. Along with this, a conscious process of institutionalization made possible the establishment of the various disciplines of social sciences. Thus, the evolution of these disciplines and their formal institutionalization has been a dynamic and continuous process, which has been in constant dialogue and debate with various other factors.

The influence of Natural Sciences has been significant to the growth and development of these upcoming disciplines. It's important to mention, at this point, that these early Social Scientists were not individuals with a radical outlook. Never-the-less, they were people who tried to obtain the scientific basis of the Study of Society. Therefore, they gave great emphasis on the need to analyze Social Life scientifically.

Auguste Comte, also known as the founder/father of Sociology, emphasized the need to analyze Society through a scientific method. This emphasis had significant importance for the development of the discipline. He revived the term, 'social physics', suggesting, thereby, that society was best studied along the model of physics. Thus, to study society, one had to be scientific, in the sense that the study should be confined "to the study of real facts, without seeking to know their first causes or final purpose".

Origin and Growth of Social Science

The Gulbenkian Report of the Commission, further, suggests that in the period of 1850-1914, clear divisions emerged between the disciplines belonging to the social sciences. There were five main places where these disciplines were institutionalized, they were, Great Britain, France, Germany, Italy and the United States. Five disciplines were accepted as belonging to social sciences. These were, history, economics, sociology, political science and anthropology. A tradition of history was already present in some form and it became the first discipline among these five to attain a degree of autonomy. Around this time, a new discipline was formed and a new name for it was coined by Comte, called, sociology. He thought that sociology would be the queen of the social sciences (perhaps like mathematics was seen as the queen of the Natural sciences). The discipline of sociology, itself, was formed through a conscious institutionalization in the second half of the 19th century. Initially, the people involved in it were those who were associated with social reform groups. This was similar to what had happened in anthropology. As it is well known, early anthropology was largely done by explorers, traders and officials of colonial regimes. The institutionalization of this discipline occurred when they were absorbed in the university system.

The human beings thought that they were capable of constructing their own laws for social and political systems. This fact, opines Wagner (1999), distinguishes that many techniques were presented by Social Science to manage post-revolutionary political situation. The mid of 18th century had observed the enlightenment of the human beings. Their tendency of being sociable and its effects on practical order of the world was central concern of Social Science. This metamorphosis into social science took place until the mid of 19th century. So, Social Science, from the beginning, has contributed in alteration of society as foreseeable. In renovating society for the advancement, Social Science has been instrumental.

How Scientific the Social Science is?

Here, it is important to discuss the development of Natural Sciences that was largely affecting the Studies of Society. Classical mechanics, which was first formulated by Newton and further, developed by Laplace and others, is seen as the foundation of science, as a whole. The influence of Newtonian thinking was so great that the upcoming Social Scientists, in their attempt to study the Society using a scientific method, plagued it with paradoxes, confusion, and unclear interpretation.

Auguste Comte, was of the view that a theoretical Science should discover the laws that govern the phenomenon which social scientists were investigating. Similarly, Durkheim, in, The Rules of Sociological Method, outlined his view of the logic and method of sociological inquiry. He argued that, the first and most fundamental rule is to consider social facts as things. Thus, the belief systems, customs and institutions of society, the facts of the social world should be considered as things, in the same way, as the objects and events of the natural world. As such, they can be directly observed and objectively measured. Although social facts enter the consciousness of individuals, i.e., the belief systems of society form a part of the outlook of its members, social facts are external to individuals. They are impressed upon them by society, they exist outside the individual and can, therefore, be studied objectively as external things. In Durkheim's view, society is not simply a collection of individuals, each was acting independently in terms of his or her particular psychology or mental state. Instead, members of society are directed by collective beliefs, values and laws, by social facts, which have an existence of their own. In Durkheim's words, 'collective ways of acting or thinking have a reality outside the individuals. Social facts, therefore, constrain individuals to behave in particular ways. The explanation of human behavior, thus, involves an examination of how that behavior is shaped by social facts. Just as the behavior of matter can be regarded as a reaction to external stimuli, so the behavior of human beings can be seen as a response to the external constraints of social facts. Given this view of the nature of human beings and society, social facts are amenable to analysis in terms of the natural science methodology.

In 1897, Durkheim's now famous work, *Suicide: A Study in Sociology* was published. Durkheim believed that this study provided the evidence to support his views on methodology outlined two years earlier in The Rules of Sociological Method. He argued that his research on suicide demonstrated that 'real laws are discoverable', that social phenomena obey laws in the same way as natural phenomena. It showed that suicide was not simply an individual act, but a product of a social force external to the individual. Its causes are to be found in society. It is the product of social facts, of 'real, living and active forces, which, because of the way they determine the individual, prove their independence of it'.

In a series of writings on suicide, the British sociologist, J. Maxwell Atkinson, rejects the logic and procedures of positivist methodology. He maintains that the social world is a construction of actors' perceptions and subjective interpretations. As such, it has no reality beyond the meanings given to it by social actors. Thus, an act of suicide is simply that which is defined as suicide by social actors. Atkinson rejects this assumption, arguing that suicide is not an objective fact that can, somehow, be separated from the perceptions of social actors. It, therefore, makes no sense for sociologists to treat suicide as facts and seek to explain their cause.

From a phenomenological perspective, therefore, the social world is a world of meaning. There is no objective reality, which lies behind that meaning. Thus, the social world is not made up of entities, which are external to the subjective experience of its members. Also, to treat its aspects as 'social facts', as 'things', is to distort and misrepresent social reality. Thus, sociologists, who treat crime and suicide as anything other than constructions of meaning, are imposing their own reality on the social world and so distorting the very reality they seek to understand.

Social Science in 20th Century

Twentieth century, believed Wagner (1999), can be marked as a century when Social Sciences got acceptance not only at political level but also at institutional level. On the onset of the 19th century, only a few institutions in Europe and North America adopted Social Sciences as an area of research and for teaching. But in contemporary times, institutes devoted to the study of society or say social world are in abundance. In 1970's, the detailed analysis and assessments of the social sciences started to re-appear with respect to epistemology, ontology and methodology of these sciences. After a lot of experiments and experiences with the social sciences, this century revealed their narrowly set limits.

Problems Faced by Social Sciences in the 20th Century

This awakening of society for Social Sciences has not been an easy process, therefore, Wagner suggests four major issues confronted by Social Sciences in that era. First issue is "rationality" of these sciences. Secondly their "usefulness" for managing or regulating power. The third issue was related to the "structure" of social sciences, whether it should have disciplinary structure or it should be inter-disciplinary based as per the need of the society. Last issue faced was the "scientific nature" of Social Sciences in accordance with the circumstances at the beginning and the end of 19th century.

The revised version of positivism appeared in the early 20th century and came to be known as logical positivism. But, nevertheless, Newtonian Scientism did receive a challenge from the theory of relativity, which was, initially, developed by, Einstein and given a new meaning by Karl Popper. The most characteristic feature that bothered Popper was the incessant stream of confirmations, of observations, which "verified" the theories in question; and this point was, constantly, emphasized by their adherents.

These factors when united made Popper take falsifiability as his foundation for separating science from non-science: if a theory is discordant with the probable experimented observations, it is deemed scientific. On the contrary, if a theory is attuned with all the empirical observations, like in Marxism, it has been altered purely to make space for such observations, or because, like in the situation of psychoanalytic concepts, it is in tandem with all the probable observations, is regarded as intuitive. However, for Popper, just because a theory has been suspected to be unscientific, doesn't necessarily uphold the fact that it is not informative and is thus, a throwaway. There exists in all possibility, the chance, that in the near future, with the advancement of technology, that very unscientific theory can be falsified.

20th century is known as Century of Social Science. Ways of thinking, particularly towards the end of eighteenth century were called as Social Science not because new questions came into existence but because a spectrum of new answers came into sight (Heilbronn et al., 1998; and earlier Therborn, 1974; Hawthorn, 1987). A lot of it is owed to American and French revolutions and that is why Wagner (1999) put it as the legacy of revolutions.

Impact of Second World War on Social Sciences

The Second World War brought landmark changes in Social Sciences. After 1945, fast changes took place in all the areas of Social Sciences. The major reasons for this were the Emergence of the U.S.A. as a major power. Hence, the political world wars were now being defined by two aspects, the cold war with the USSR and the self-assertion by the known European countries. This was the time when the university system was being getting expanded in all parts of the world. The academia received and used these universities as a platform for experimentation and generation of knowledge in the field of Social Sciences.

Behaviorism and Social Sciences

Irrespective of the adulation amassed by Popper's Open Society and its opponents during the 2nd World War, the effect of determinism was unshakable, even in the post war period. The Behaviorism approach (unlike the behaviorism of the learning theory) in political science quests for an objective, quantified approach that strives to define and anticipate political behavior.

This approach is associated with the ascent of behavioral sciences and has taken shape from the natural sciences. Before the ascent of the behavioral revolution, political science's standing as a science was undecided, for the critics believed that political science lacked a scientific method of study and is overly qualitative and normative, hence, unfit to be deemed as a science. On the other hand, behaviorist methodology and empirical research were austere enough to confirm their study as a social science.

He described Behaviorism in the following words: "Behaviorism was not a clearly defined movement for those who were thought to be behaviorists. It was more clearly definable by those who were opposed to it, because they were describing it in terms of the things within the newer trends that they found objectionable. So, some would define behaviorism as an attempt to apply the methods of natural sciences to human behavior. Some others would define it as an excessive emphasis upon quantification. Another group of scholars would define it as individualistic reductionism. From the inside, the practitioners were of different minds as what it was that constituted behaviorism, and a few were in agreement."

Other scholars have pointed out that science and culture have become closely associated in the post-modern period, most noticeably in the way that the Chaos Theory and deconstruction subvert the dominant values of established paradigms. TR Young identifies similarities between the Chaos Theory and Post Modernism in Chaos and Science: Metaphysics of the Postmodern (1991) arguing that the Chaos Theory 'decenters' determinism, certainty, coherence and order from primacy in science and, therefore, that it is compatible with the indeterminate parameters of the Post Modern culture. He suggests that the chaos theory displaces 'all claims of perfection, finality, normality or historical necessity' form the elevated, unquestioned positions in a similar manner to Post Modernism and argues, from this, that the Chaos Theory provides 'an elegant theoretical envelope in which to locate Post Modern Science.

The Gulbenkian Commission (1996) had appropriately pointed out that World War-II: the first thing to note is where this institutionalization took place. There were five main locales for social science activity during the nineteenth century: Great Britain, France, the Germanys, Italy, and the United States. Most of the scholars and most of the universities (of course, not all) were located in these five places. The universities, in other countries, lacked the numerical weight or international prestige of those in these five. To this day, most of the nineteenth-century works that we still read, were written in one of these five locales. These names, as we shall discuss, were, primarily, five: history, economics, sociology, political science, and anthropology. One might add to this list, as we shall see, the so-called Oriental Sciences (called Orientalism in English), despite the fact that they self-consciously did not consider themselves social sciences. Why we do not include geography, psychology, and law in this list?

The Gulbenkian report (1996) ends with a short commentary on the future of the social sciences. The members believe that multidisciplinary work has come to stay, even as they recognize, that due to the problem of resources, there will be constant tension between new disciplines being formed and the consolidation of the established disciplines. Also, they strongly feel that multidisciplinary work must be institutionalized in various ways, such as offering appointments to faculty in more than one department and having students attached to different departments. This formal movement from one discipline to another constitutes an important mark of liberal education.

Social Sciences in India

Alex M. George and Amman Madan (2009) Social Sciences in Indian schools states that Social Sciences are, in an in-enviable position. On the one hand, they are expected to shoulder the bulk of the normative expectations from schooling thus, they are supposed to teach everything from a commitment to keeping the streets clean to the internalization of a pluralist vision of the nation. Yet, they are treated as step-sisters of science. Science is seen as a solid grounding for a lucrative career, while social sciences are considered soft, trivial and for the weak. It puts the social sciences at the Centre of a struggle over the purpose and meaning of schooling-is schooling only about getting a job or to become a better person.

In India, we have over-emphasized the institutional structure. We have very limited number of research journals and publishers in the field of social sciences. On the others hand, our university system is not opened-up to the needs of social science research. Our university system does not agree to inter-disciplinary or multi-disciplinary movement of faculty or researchers, so as to encourage social science research for teaching. The Indian bureaucratic model of educational institutions is always burdened with undue interference of ideologies and agendas. Our universities are still considering natural sciences as an important area of research at the same time, social sciences as well as humanities, are treated as step children.

Social-science and Natural sciences have never been compartmentalized, as there has always been the influence of sciences over social-science. Throughout our attempts of discovering a science of society to the present day, it would not be an exaggeration to say that a science of society is possible. By the science of society, we do not mean devising universal laws or rules of Society, which would help, predict the future, but it should be to help in understanding society. The encyclopedia clarifies the social science in their decisions: the purely social-science, the semi social sciences and the sciences with social implications. Social Science is waiting for its Newton. Peter Wagner (1999) Twentieth Century – the century of the social sciences and we have seen tremendous growth in the last three decades and we are expecting much more.

To make people realize the potential of social sciences we as teachers and teacher educators are required to explore the field of social sciences with the help of research and writing. Keeping this in mind let's explore the meaning, nature, growth, significance, pedagogic techniques and the various other facets of one the social science subject—Political Science.

2

Political Science as a Discipline of Knowledge

The human society is a complex structure and for the existence and maintenance of society the individuals who are a part of it are required to be aware of its basic elements and its functioning. In order to maintain the essence of a particular society, individuals are also required to follow certain rules and regulations and submit to an authority which can be trusted. The subject of Political Science is a social science discipline which makes an individual aware of how some of the essential functions in of the society are performed and how people govern and are governed in the societal set up.

Meaning and Nature of Political Science

Though known by several names as 'politics'(Aristotle), 'political science'(William Godwin & others), 'science of state' (R.G. Gettell) and 'science of politics' (Sir Frederick Pollock) this subject lacks a precise nomenclature.

In very simple terms, it is defined as a study of state and government. The English word 'politics' originates from the Greek word viz. Polis (city states), Polity (government) and Politela (constitution).

Political Science is a discipline which deals with the study of the state, nation, government, politics and policies of government. Aristotle defined it as the study of the state. It deals extensively with the theory and practice of politics, and the analysis of political systems, political behavior and political culture. Political Science intersects with other fields, including economics, law, sociology, history, anthropology, public administration, public policy, national politics, international relations, comparative politics, psychology, political organization and political theory. (Thomas. R. Dye, 2016)

Although it was codified in the 19th century, when all the social sciences were established, Political Science has ancient roots as, it originated almost 2,500 years ago with the works of Plato and Aristotle. The term Political Science is intimately related to the word "Politics", which itself is derived from the Greek word, "Polis", that means a city-state, the general form of political organization in ancient Greece. The origin of political thought in the west, therefore, goes back to Greece.

Science or Art

To be briefly summarized, this controversy can be dealt as like when politics as such in the original Greek sense, is a study of the city state and its administration in practical as well as philosophical terms. However, the point of difficulty at this stage is that the term 'politics' is taken by many as both a science and an art. The difficulty is further increased when we take note of the fact the ever since Hobbes identified it with 'power' and Auguste Comte popularized the trend of 'positivism'/ 'reductionism'. The original Greek meaning of 'politics' became outdated.

Further, it is to be noted that as other subjects like physics has made much development since the time of Galileo and Newton to Einstein and Economics has much changed from the days of Adam smith and Marshal to those of Keynes and hicks, so has political science under gone significant shifts and changes from the times of Plato and Aristotle in ancient to those of Laski and Lasswell in present times.

A peculiar feature of this development is to be traced in the fact that social sciences have borrowed much from natural sciences in the present century (20th) owing to their craze for 'scientism'.

The result is that, like other social sciences, political science has also been 'scientised' to some extent. It has had its own impact on changing the character of the subject from a largely normative into a largely empirical sense.

In order to study the evolution and growth of politics and political science, it is essential for us to understand the various approaches towards the discipline as when the time went by.

Historical Approach

The traditional/historical approach to political science is best represented by G.H.Sabine. He proceeds in a very practical manner. He suggests that we include in political science all those subjects which have been the major themes of discussion in the writings of well known political philosopher like Plato, Aristotle, Hobbes, Locke, Rousseau, Bentham, Mill, Green, Hegel, Marx and others. In the writings of these philosophers we may try to search out those questions which they have raised about the truth and validity of political theories. A political theory according to Sabine is always advanced in a "pretty specific situation" and therefore, reconstruction of the time, place and circumstances in which it was produced is essential to understand. However, it is futuristic too in a sense that this theory excels both in "analysis of a present situation and in suggesting for other situation". Such a good political theory has significance for all times to come.

Sociological Approach

The historical approach has been generally criticised as one which is too much deferential to tradition. It is also blamed to take a narrow view of politics and restricts it to the domain of the state.

Several contemporary writers have sought to widen the scope of political science so as to include not only the state but the society as well. For example, George and E.G. Catlin, would like to use politics in the Aristotelian sense to include all those activities which are carried out within the auspices of the society.

Catlin regards political science as indistinguishable from sociology and has pointed out a number of advantages of this approach:-

- It allows one to deal with the relations and structure of society as a whole and not with a segment of it artificially created which can be described as "state".
- It links up his studies with a general theory of society which political scientists cannot ignore.
- If truly an analysis has to be done, this approach allows the scope for analysis of the basic characteristics so as to study not only institutions but processes as well.

This approach would then include within the scope of study of political science. The study of power and influence or as max Weber would say "the struggle for power or the influencing of those in power". Closely connected in the understanding that it is control which links up the two poles of freedom and authority and play in political science the role that demand, supply and competitive price play in economics.

Philosophical Approach

Besides the traditional (historical) and contemporary (sociological approach), there is a third view point advanced by Leo Strauss known as the philosophical approach. Leo Strauss makes a distinction between political theory and political philosophy as parts of political thought.

According to Strauss, political theory is an attempt to truly know the nature of political things. Political philosophy includes an attempt to know the nature of political things as well as to know what right/good political order is. Political theory and philosophy are complementary. So, Leo Strauss would reject both historicism of Sabine and social science positivism (reductionism) of Catlin as "the serious antagonisms of political philosophy".

Values would thus, form an indispensable part of political philosophy and cannot be excluded from study of politics. Also, the distinction between philosophy and science cannot be applied to study of human affairs. So, there can neither be a non-philosophical political science nor a non scientific political philosophy.

What is the true scope of Political Science?

To put it in simplistic terms, it can therefore be stated that political science seeks to include the study of the 'state as it has been', 'state as it is' and 'state as it ought to be'. In short, its scope extends to the study of all phases of the state.

a) *State as it has been*: In the first instance, political science makes a survey of the origin and growth of organized political life. It starts with the consideration of the evolution of political life from simple to complex.
   Since early times, the scholar made attempt to draw inference and draw tentative conclusions about the state, government, law and political behavior. Thus, they helped in the growth of various currents of political thought. The study of past has been of great help in understanding the present.
b) *State as it is*: Politics and more precisely political science makes an empirical investigation of existing political institutions and phenomenon. It also examines prevailing concepts and the group/organizations which seek power and influence the society.
   At present, the state is intimately linked with other states and deals also with various international organization and the rules

of international conducts, popularly known as international law.

This has broadened the scope of political science, because now it concerns the study of international bodies. Also, in recent times the development of behavioral approach, studies of opinion polls and election studies have also fallen within the scope of political science.

c) *State as it should be*: Finally, political science tries to arrive at practical decision about the policy to be adopted on the basis of the past experience and the current working of the political institution.

The existing development and the tendencies are studied with a view to predict the likely course of development in the future. Efforts are also made to make proposals for modification in the existing political structure and process to make them more effective. In short, political science helps to explain the past of the state to understand the present and to direct its future.

Thus, political speculation has been an important aspect of political science since the earliest times and the still continues to important part of it.

Study of Power

In recent years, the scope of political science has been considerably widened and many other aspects have been added. One such aspect is study of power. In recent times, Scholars like Lasswell, Kaplan, Morgenthauetc has started to study politics from the angle of power. They have asserted that since, it is the element of power that distinguishes the state from other associations, this is important.

New Meaning of Political Science

In recent years, scholars have preferred to use the term 'politics' over political science and viewed it as a struggle for power. Lasswell and Kaplan view politics as "the study of the shaping and sharing of power". It is held that "politics is organised dispute about power and its use involving choice among competing values, ideas, interests and demands".

It can be said that scholars who view politics as the study of power argue that this change has resulted in broadening the area of inquiry and made political analysis more realistic. This has two distinct advantages over the earlier approaches/methods of study.

Firstly, it includes the study of not only the legal and formal but also the 'extra- legal' and 'informal' processes involved. Secondly, it pays more attention to political man as a base unit of analysis. At this point we may end on the concluding note that even Aristotle, the father of political science had described 'human as a political animal.'

Interdisciplinary Nature of Political Science

Political Science includes the study of state and the nation and neither the state nor the nation can be taught in isolation. Thus, the scope of social sciences and especially Political Science is very wide because it includes the knowledge of every sphere of life as may be called social, political, economic, religious, cultural, psychological, philosophical etc.

Political Science, is thus, not a separate and independent discipline but is only a part of the social sciences. Systematic studies of institutions and functioning of human society, man's behavior in society and the interpersonal relationships of individuals as members of society are called social sciences. (Gauba, 2000)

Political Science, being a social science discipline is interdisciplinary by nature which implies that it draws upon and contributes to other social disciplines or branches of knowledge and thus dependent on them in various ways. It includes-

- *Study of Cause and Effect Relationship*: In our present day life every event or happening is the result of the efforts done in the past. Our social, economic, geographical, cultural and political conditions are the results of the human activities as well as the environmental activities of the past and the practices of the present will affect the conditions in the future. The chain of cause and effect will go on from decade to decade. Due to this relationship, we can call it as a science because science also relates with cause and effect as well as what is and what ought to be. In the same way with the help of social science pupil will be able to understand the present conditions and their cause and also to predict the future of the world.
- *A study of Human Relationships*: The relationship between the human beings can be studied under the following heads-

  a) People and People
  b) People and institutions

c) People and earth
d) People and goods

This explains that a peaceful world is based upon mutual respect and understanding, the relationships of people and people and people and institutions are explained with the help of civics. The goals for students is to achieve in Political Science are to integrate school and society by taking an active role in social institutions, reveal pattern of behaviour indicating democracy as a way of life such as accepting and valuing others.

- *Study of Human and its Surroundings:* The scope of social science is the study of human, its way of living, present and past, her/his significant achievements, her/his institutions and problems of life S/he faces with the increased amount of information pertaining to new items and happenings reported in different media, it helps the learners to become proficient in identifying the places where the events took place.
- *Study of Society:* The subject matter of social science consists of the different traditions, customs, rituals, and ideas of the society developed from the ancient period to the present time. The society starts from the family and goes on to the international level.
- *Functional Study of Natural Sciences*: Social Science and Natural Sciences are interrelated and interdependent. The amount and thoughts and complexities of knowledge in the social sciences are vastly greater than in natural sciences. Although, man has built a great material civilization, s/he has not been able to apply her/his reason to solve the problems of a complex industrial age. Only through the application of reason and thoughts, the social scientists will be able to extend the boundaries of knowledge and many devise methods that will end the lag in social process. Scientists get ideas from the society for their inventions and discoveries will be proved only when they are applicable in the society.

To sum up, political science is related to all social sciences. Its study is incomplete without realizing its relationship with other social sciences. It is maintaining its separate identity but it will have to work in close cooperation with other disciplines in social sciences for successful outcome of educational efforts.

Relationship of Political Science with other Social Science Subjects

The various social science subjects are closely related to each other and are dependent on each other. Here we will analyze how Political Science is intricately linked with the other social science disciplines such as History, Geography, Economics, Sociology, Psychology and Philosophy.

Political Science and History

History and Political Science are often described as sister subjects. The use of history is significant for the study of Political Science.

History deals with past events, movements, revolutions, national struggles etc. The historical facts and data which include information about significant events, individuals and cultures, helps in understanding various political phenomenon and the working of various political institutions and political thought.

John Seeley (1834-95) explained the close relationship between the two subjects and stated that 'History without Political Science has no fruit; Political Science without history has no root'. This statement highlights how both the disciplines helps in the growth and understanding of each other.

Montesquieu and Bryce made use of historical materials to study Political Science. Lord Bryce claims that, Political Science stands midway between history and politics, between the past and the present. It has drawn its materials from the one; it has to apply them to the other. (Bryce, 1909)

In order to understand any political system, thinker, institution and so on we are required to look at the past time in which they existed and understand things in a historical context. Historical analysis also helps in learning about the past achievements as well as the mistakes and this helps in improving the present political system.

When various Political Science' concepts, ideologies, terms and issues are discussed then their historical development is also taken into consideration.

Political Science and Economics

The ancient Greeks regarded economics to be a sub division of Political Science.

Economics deals with the study of how resources are produced, allocated, and distributed. Modern discipline of Economics originated from classical political economy. Political economy is an interdisciplinary field which makes use of a combination of economics, law, and political science in explaining how political institutions, the political environment, and the economic system capitalist, socialist, or mixed influence each other.

The mainstream economics approach of rational choice has been applied in fields that were previously the exclusive domain of either sociology or political science. Within political science the field of study has also been extended to cover not only the traditional domain of the state and governmental policies but rather collective action in general, including organisation, mobilization and discourse. (Stavros Ioannides, 2007)

A large portion of politics is about how government can influence the economy. The study of these economic effects relate to political science. As we know that Political science is concerned with the state, government, agencies, etc. So, Economics has to do with the system. The close relationship between the two subjects can also be understood by looking at Kautilya's Arthsastra (4th century B.C.) which is one of the most influential treatises in Political Science and Economics in the Indian Civilization. This work deals with virtually all aspects of governance in a monarchical state. It focuses on state power, its acquisition, exercise and disruption. It elaborates that how the statecraft, the economic policy and the military strategy should be given equal significance for the proper functioning of the state.

From the Arthashastra, it becomes clear that it is significant to study the influence of the economic set up of a country on its political structure and vice-versa, so it is significant to include the elements of economics in the study of Political Science. As Political Science also lays stress on the study of power relations in the society so we also need to see how the people in power make use of the resources and how they are distributed among others. Both Political scientists and economists rely on the study of both the subjects so as to get a clearer picture of the society. So we cannot ignore the prevalence for a close relationship between the two subjects.

Political Science and Sociology

The mother of social sciences sociology has a close relationship with other social science subjects. Auguste Compte, the father of sociology regarded Sociology as the science of society. Sociology focuses on how the social system operates and how the social order is maintained or altered. In order to understand society in its totality its significant to study how the society is maintained or changed and what are the rules that helps in the protection of social order, this is where the significance of Political Science creeps in. Just like the other social science subjects, Sociology and Political Science also share a close relation. According to Morris Ginsberg "Historically, Sociology has its main roots in politics and philosophy of history". The state, which is the center of political science in its early stage, was more of a social than political institution. (Bhushan Sachdeva, 2012)

Political science and sociology are inter-related, political scientists and sociologists contribute mutually for the benefit of society as a whole. For example, the institution of marriage and related problems after that, namely divorce are within the domain of sociology. How to solve these problems in a harmonious way for better standard of life is within the competence of political science. What was once a sub-field of sociology has now takes the form of "political sociology" which is now a legitimate subfield of political science.

Political Science and Geography

There is a close relation between Political Science and Geography. "Geo" refers to earth and "graphy" means description. So the description of the earth is known as Geography. It is the science of "the earth's surface, form, physical features, natural and political divisions, climate, production, population" and so on.

The geographical conditions and the physical environment impacts the character and national life of a country and the national policies and functioning of the government is also largely dependent on the geographical conditions and also the natural resources available in the country.

A political investigator studies Geography with a view to knowing the influence of the geographical conditions and the physical environment on Politics and Political Science. Geo-politics gives the useful information regarding the study of the origin and growth of political institutions.

In modern times considerable attention has been paid by a number of writers to the influence of geographical factors on political institutions. There researches and writings have contributed to give "political geography", a name—"Geopolitics.

Geo-politics deals with "the application of political and economic geography to the external problems of states, notably problems of national power, frontiers and possibilities for expansion." Since territory is an essential feature of a state, geo-political factors naturally influence political activities and national politics.

Politics of many countries and their international relations are dependent on their geographical locations and their natural resources. In the past we have seen how the international relations, growth, development and peace of a country are altered on the basis of availability and sharing of various natural resources within the country and with other countries. So the study of geographical aspects is significant to understand the political state of various countries in their totality.

Political Science and Philosophy

Political Science and Philosophy share a lot with each other. Philosophy as a field of study primarily centers around values which are linked to the wisdom imparting domains. Initially, Political Science was called Political Philosophy. Study of philosophy of State i.e. Political Thought is a part of the study of Political Science. Philosophy provides to Political Science knowledge of ideal human behavior, political values, good and bad in political theory, right and wrong laws, policies and governmental decisions and theory of ideal social-political institutions. Philosophy also studies ideal political behavior, good political values, ideal political institutions and ideal political conduct. Ideal political reforms and political ideologies Individualism liberalism socialism, communism and others. It is a part of the study of Political Science. Each political ideology is a particular and distinct philosophy of state.

From Philosophy, Political Science gets its value laden concepts and the normative leanings, which can be studied in the sub field of political science, i.e. Political Theory. Political theory focuses on the "oughts" and the "should" aspect. Where political science deals with the scientific, empirical and, political theory clearly is a politically customized version of philosophy where the political ideas and concepts are studied, which act as a guiding tool of how the political and social structure ought to be organized and aspirations are given a clear directions. This shows that Political Science and Philosophy share a close relationship.

Political Science and Psychology

Psychology deals with the study of the behavior of man and what causes are there behind such a behavior. It enquires into the mind of man and explains the motives of human action. Political Science, which deals with the political relationship of human beings, cannot ignore the psychological effects.

The State and its political institutions are the products of the human mind and can best be understood in terms of the mind. Theories about political conduct that are not grounded in an adequate psychology are apt to be defective.

Many political scientists are of the opinion that there exists a close relationship between the two subjects. According to Woodsworth, Political Science formulates its theories on the basis of the conclusions arrived at by psychology about the behavior of men.

Barker says, "The application of the psychological clue to the riddles of human activity has indeed become the fashion of the day. If our forefathers thought biologically, we think psychologically."

The affinity between Political Science and Psychology has been greatly emphasized during recent times. Gabriel Tarde, Le Bon MacDougall, Graham Wallas, and Baldwin are the prominent writers who have given psychological explanations of almost all the political problems.

The discipline of political psychology further explains the close connection between the two subjects. Political psychology is an interdisciplinary academic field dedicated to understanding politics, politicians and political behavior from a psychological perspective. The relationship between politics and psychology is considered bi-directional, with psychology being used as a lens for understanding politics and politics being used as a lens for understanding psychology.

Integrated Approach to Teach Political Science

In the NCERT Self Instructional Package for Upper Primary Teachers (2003), the concept and uses of the integrated approach are clearly elaborated. It is stated that in order to make teaching effective the teacher adopts various transactional strategies of teaching social sciences. The most commonly used approach is to teach history, geography, economics and other social sciences separately as independent subjects. This approach is referred as the subject matter approach. Proponents of this approach argue that separate subjects have their own inherent worth. The subject based approach is most commonly used approach in schools. Though this approach has many advantages, it suffers from a major drawback of providing fragmented knowledge to students.

In contrast the integrated approach which is recently gaining momentum, strongly advocates that social science courses can be transacted more meaningfully through an integrated approach drawing knowledge from various academic disciplines.

The integrated approach is considered as a viable alternative to overcome the limitations of the subject based approach. Under this approach the themes become the central focus and students are encouraged to pursue it holistically, drawing information from various subject areas. This approach, therefore helps to develop a holistic perspective of various issues, relating them to real life problems, thereby developing problem solving skills among students.

Integration refers to the possibility that the curriculum is defined more in terms of student's needs so that different teachers in different subject areas may be said to be teaching the same thing.

The word 'integration' has been used by some writers to a particular kind of interrelationship between subject matter, while others take it more loosely to cover a wide variety of ways combining subjects. Some for instance, would regard linking course in literature, history, music, etc by covering the same time span in relation to each as a form of integration, while others may not accept as truly integrated curriculum anything that did not break down the very notion of distinct subjects and provide opportunity to the study of a particular issue from a multidisciplinary point of view.

In a truly integrated approach, therefore, the subject matter boundaries blur and even disappear; students are encourage to pursue topics holistically drawing from various subject areas. Here, real life problems or topics that are meaningful and interesting to students become more pertinent, and disciplines are treated as mere tools that help students understand and solve the problem. Consequently, the syllabus following an integrated approach is arranged according to themes, or fundamental issues and problems.

The genesis of emphasis on integrated approach in India may be traced in the 'Curriculum for Ten Year School: A Framework (1975)', which suggested three options for teaching social sciences. These were as follows:

1. History, geography and civics could be taught as separate subjects at the middle and high schools. Economics may be added as a separate subject at the secondary stage.

2. History and geography may be kept in one section and the other section may include civics and economics. Both these sections can be taught is classes 6-10.
3. History, geography, civics and economics may be taught in an integrated manner in classes 6-10.

The NCERT followed the first approach which continued till recently. In this approach the students and teachers have been facing a number of problems. The course content is too vast and the students are generally unable to see the interrelationship among various subjects.

The NCF (2000) emphasized on the integrated approach for teaching social sciences. It is felt that since the social problems are multifaceted and multidimensional, they need multi-dimensional solution taking help of various academic disciplines whenever and wherever required. It is expected that the integrated approach will not only help in reducing the curriculum load but also making it more relevant to students by selecting and organizing content into themes. The thematic approach of integration provides enough scope to draw content from various subject areas to show the multidimensional nature of a problem and its solution.

Aims and Objectives of Teaching Political Science at Secondary/ Senior Secondary School Level in India

The main aim of teaching Political Science in a Democratic Secular Country is to make the citizens of the country respect, preserve and protect the democratic ideals of liberty, equality, justice and sovereignty.

The CBSE Senior Secondary Curriculum 2015-16, Main Subject Volume 1 states the following objectives of teaching Political Science at the Senior Secondary level. The curriculum highlights that at the "senior secondary level students who opt for Political Science are given an opportunity to get introduced to the diverse concerns of a Political Scientist. At this level there is a need to enable students to engage with political processes that surround them and provide them with an understanding of the historical context that has shaped the present. The different courses introduce the students to the various streams of the discipline of Political Science: Political Theory, Indian Politics and International Politics. Concerns of the other two streams - Comparative Politics and Public Administration- are accommodated at different places in these courses. In introducing these streams, special care has been taken not to burden the students with the current jargon of the discipline. The basic idea here is to lay the foundations for a serious engagement with the discipline at the under graduation stage.

Objectives of Teaching various Streams of Political Science

Indian Constitution at Work

- Enable students to understand the historical processes and the circumstances in which the Constitution was drafted. Provide opportunity for students to become familiar with the diverse visions that guided the makers of the Indian Constitution.
- Enable students to identify certain key features of the Constitution and compare these to other constitutions in the world.
- Analyse the ways in which the provisions of the Constitution have worked in real political life.

1. Political Theory
    - Develop the skills for logical reasoning and abstraction. Inculcate attention to and respect for viewpoints other than one's own.
    - Introduce students to the different political thinkers in relation to a concept and in everyday social life.
    - Enable students to meaningfully participate in and develop internal concerns of the political life that surrounds them.
    - Encourage the students to analyse any unexamined prejudices that one may have inherited.
2. Contemporary World Politics
    - Enable the students to expand their horizons beyond India and make sense of the political map of contemporary world.
    - Familiarise the students with some of the key political events and processes in the post-cold war era. Equip students to be conscious of the way in which global events and processes shape our everyday lives.
    - Strengthen their capacity for political analysis by thinking of contemporary developments in a historical perspective.

3. Politics in India after Independence
    - Enable students to become familiar with some of the key political events and figures in the post-independence period.
    - Develop skills of political analysis through an understanding of events and processes of recent history. Develop their capacity to link macro processes with micro situations and their own life.
    - Encourage the students to take a historical perspective of making sense of contemporary India. (CBSE, 2015)

As per the NCERT, the main aims and objectives of teaching Political Science at the Secondary level is to introduce students to some of the important ideas and concepts which form a part of the living tradition of political thought in the world.

Previously, students were exposed to political ideas and theories primarily through the study of political ideologies, such as, Liberalism, Marxism, or Fascism. Concepts like freedom and equality entered the picture only indirectly in terms of their place in a given system of ideas. In the new course the central focus is on concepts rather than ideologies.

The study of Political Theory is aimed at not only making students learn about the ideas which have been developed by thinkers over the ages but also to be able to respond to them on the basis of their own experience of the world. They are able to refine their ideas and express them with greater precision and clarity and they are able to critically reflect on their beliefs and ideas and offer reasoned and compelling arguments in defense of their position.

Students are also made to study the Politics of our own country. The study of the working of the Indian Constitution is employed to be a gateway to studying politics in India. The study of Indian politics is a window to understand politics in other societies. Through the study of institutions and the politics of power surrounding them, students would come to know about the principles and theories of politics.

Evolution and Growth of Political Science

The topic of 'evolution and growth of political science' is a very challenging task indeed, for to capture the growth and evolution of a discipline, which is as old as civilization itself, is probably beyond the scope of any single study.

However, it is a fascinating ride through the roller coaster of the science of politics or philosophy of politics is discussed here here.

For the purpose of clarity, it is important that methodology should be discussed with the readers. As mentioned above, to capture the evolution of political science and its growth till present times is a gigantic task. There had the option of either taking a chronological look at the process, which we did not because then the study would have lost its scope, somewhere amidst the highs and lows or the contours of this extremely fascinating but very complex discipline.

Instead, we chose to adopt a rather integrated approach, in the sense we seek to study the change in the nature of the scope/ boundaries of political science. Through this, an attempt is made to briefly capture the essence of the developments within the discipline.

In short, and in its simplistic explanation, it is to be kept in the back of our minds that political science like other social sciences (economics, sociology, history, anthropology, psychology etc.) has been born out of the mother discipline of Philosophy.

Within the political thought since the time of Plato and Aristotle to Machiavelli, Hobbes, Locke to Marx and Laski and LasswelL, Morgenthau to Rawls, Nozick, Samuel Huntington, of today political science has emerged from being a philosophy (political thought and theory) towards a scientific drive under the behavioristic school of thought or may we say a wave (David Easton & others) to the post-behavioral revolution of reconciliation, may, an integration of/ recognition and acceptance of indispensability of facts and value from the preview of a social science.

In this attempt to tend a strong element of science to the social studies the very nature and definition of what is a science or what elements comprise a science have undergone a change or we would say a reform.

What is Science after all?

Let us have a brief look at this issue to the literal meaning of 'knowledge', this word science, on account of its close association with the physical science like physics, chemistry etc. has acquired a special meaning of being a body of exact knowledge or principles capable of explaining every relevant phenomenon in the selected field and so uniform that it should be possible to make predictions on this basis so as to future happenings and events.

It is obvious that the political science or for that matter any social sciences cannot produce results with same certainty because the basis of their focus is a human being which is such a dynamic component.

Social scientists would argue that this is indeed not a true test of science. In fact, the scientific character of any study depends on its methodology other than the exactness or certainty which its predictions can attain.

It is true that the human behavior can be subjected to same uniformities of nature to which the physical word is subject. Human behavior can never be classified, studied and also generalize upon. These generalization do not have a cent percent validity like the formulae, theorems of physical sciences but they are useful probabilities.

Thus, when we adopt the second approach, it is concluded that indeed a science of politics is possible and has infact been evolved over time. It may yet be centuries behind the levels of maturation which physical sciences have achieved in a sense, yet, the empirical character of scientific enquiry involved in their process of study are very much relevant.

And else, more importantly in a way no social sciences and more particularly political science does not attempt to become a 'pure science', either (in the sense of physical science) because at the base of it, the attempt is to study the human behavior and not a mechanistic, value free physical world.

Also on the other hand, it is the physical and environment sciences more particularly which are trying to adopt a more humane and socially integrated outlook towards their own discipline.

Political science, in mid twentieth century is a discipline in search of its identity. Through the efforts to solve this identity crisis it has begun to show evidence of emerging as an autonomous and independent discipline with a systematic theoretical structure of its own. The factor that has contributed most to this end has been the reception integration of the methods of science into the core of the discipline.

Introduction: David Easton

Disciplines originate and grow over a period of time. New researches are made and new dimension are added. Similarly, conceptions regarding the nature and scope of political science have changed from time to time. Aristotle, who laid down the beginnings of political science had used the term politics in a sufficiently broad sense so as to cover the 'polis' or the state, the structure of the family, the control of slaves, the monopoly of revolutions and comments on pure democracy.

George E.G. Catlin writes in Gould and thrush edited 'Contemporary Political Thought' about the issues, scope, value and direction. For Aristotle, politics included national polities, municipal and international polities, patriarchy and the structure of trade unions or the employee organizations.

A definition of this kind could be accepted when political science was the 'master science' as Aristotle had conceived it as science which gave knowledge and understanding to those who controlled the 'polis' and enable them to co-ordinate to other activities in society with a view to providing good life for those who comprises it. As the state activities became restricted in its activities and other social sciences took shape, there was a need for a narrower conceptual framework and a precise definition of political science.

Political science now became the 'science of the state' or a 'branch of the social sciences dealing with the theory, organization, government and practice of the state' with its emphasis generally on the state and its sub-units as governing structure and was studied from a legal institutional perspective.

With the growth of economics, sociology psychology and anthropology as a separate sciences in the nineteenth century, it became necessary to distinguish political science from them in clearer terms.

Growth of Political Science in India

The study of Politics is not a new development in India, it can be traced back to ancient times. The Rig Veda, Samhitas, Brahamans and Buddhist Pali Canyons have highlighted the significance of the study of politics. Chanakya (c.350-275 bc), one of the earliest Indian political thinker, who wrote the famous Arthashastra was also a teacher of Political Science.

In the article, 'Political Science in India: A discipline and intellectual pursuit', Ghanshyam Shah has explained that "Political Science as an academic discipline in modern education system as we understand today, was introduced in America in Columbia College in 1880. The objective of teaching then was the formation of moral character of individuals and training for participation in public life as ministers and members of executive."

Before independence, Political Science did not emerge as a separate discipline in India, for a long time it was being taught as a part of history. The colonizers/British rulers at that time did not encourage the study of politics and various political institutions. (Bains, 1971)

The academicians of history were also not in favour of giving political science the status of a separate discipline. They had their personal interest as making political science a separate discipline would have reduced the domain of history. Besides history, some other subjects have also considered political science as their subsidiary and consequently dominated it for a long time. In some universities political science courses formed an integral part of the curriculum in Economics and the syllabus of these courses was, therefore, drawn up by the latter department.

In others, Philosophy occupied such a position. In some cases even Sociology enjoyed a pre-eminent position. The result was that the development of studies in political science could not take place independently but only within the confines of the parent discipline. That is why in such cases the establishment of separate departments in political science was delayed and the subject neglected. (Bains, 1971)

"The Britishers made sure that no study of political phenomenon could be carried out in the country as it would eventually help in the movement for India's freedom. Most of the courses were aimed at a study of India's constitutional development, British constitutional history, Western political ideas and International relations. The latter was more or less a study of modern European history. A study of Indian nationalism did not find a deserved place in the curriculum. Therefore there was hardly any university which provided a course on political thinking in modern India. (S. V. Kogekar and A. Appadorai, Political Science in India Delhi, Premier Publishing Co, 1953), p. 11, as quoted in Bains, 1971)"

In 1943, the sixth annual session of the Indian Political Science Association was held in Lucknow, where several papers on courses of studies in Political Science in Indian Universities were contributed by the members. Through this it became clear that they seemed to be unanimously of the view that the Indian political science curriculum was blindly based on the traditions of the older British universities. The curriculum did not cater to the needs of

India and was based entirely on the experience of the Western countries. (Kogekar and Appadorai, op. cit, p. 16: as quoted in Bains, 1971)

"Indians were not able to make any contribution in any sphere of political studies. They had to depend entirely on books and authoritative materials and commentaries written by foreign scholars. Except one or two commentaries, we do not come across any standard work on India's national movement written during the period before independence by an Indian political scientist. No doubt a number of books were written but these were either a rehash of what had been written by someone else or were poor in quality and whatever was of acceptable standard was produced by those other than political scientists." (K.P. Karunakaran, Studies on the Indian National Movement: A Trend Report ICSSR, mimeo. (1970) as quoted in Bains, 1971)

Things took a different shape with India's Independence. The new government realized the significance of education and gave it top priority. "A large number of universities and institutes of higher education were set up and in 20 years their number rose five-fold. From 17 in 1947, the number of universities increased to 85 by 1968. (G. K. Ojha, *The Teaching of Social Sciences in India* (Delhi, Universal Book & Stationary Co., 1968), pp. 215-21. As quoted in Bains, 1971). With such efforts the discipline of Political Science also received encouragement. A number of universities opened departments of political science. In 1938, it was reported, only five universities had independent departments of political science. (Gurmukh Nihal Singh in S.A.H. Haqqi, The Indian Political Science Association 1938-63 (A Jigarh, 196 \3), p. 1. As quoted in Bains, 1971). This number was increased to 15 by the year 1951. (Kogekar and Appadorai, op. cit. 9 pp. 54-55. As quoted in Bains, 1971) In 1967 the University Grants Commission reported the establishment of full-fledged departments of political science in 36 universities. (UGC. Review Committee Report op. cit, V, pp. 8–9. As quoted in Bains, 1971)) As of the year 1971 the number has gone to 59.11 Independence also brought new responsibilities and created avenue for careers in administration and active politics. (11. B.S. Khanna, Survey of Research in Public Administration at the Union and State Levels, ICSSR (Mimeo), 1971, p. I, This excludes five separate departments of Public Administration as quoted in Bains, 1971).

Prabhat Kumar Datta in his article, 'Political Science in India: An Enquiry into the Present state of the discipline' elaborated the growth of Political Science in our country and stated that

"In Indian context its roots can be traced back to several centuries. As an academic discipline its appearance is, however, a recent phenomenon. The discipline was formally born in 1930s after an institutional rupture with history, and appropriated a part of its area of enquiry. The north India pioneered the new breakaway discipline designated as 'Politics' (Raghavendra Rao, K. 'Political Science in India: A Marxist Project' in State and Society, Second Quarter, 1984, p. 63. As quoted in Datta, 1989). Initially the growth was very slow. Upto 1938 only 5 universities had offered courses in political science. (Datta, 1989)

After the Second World War, as the American Methodological Invasion took place, the discipline took a new shape throughout the globe with the interventions and inputs made by American political scientists. "New conceptual frameworks and research methods focused on Behavioralism challenged the centuries-old knowledge of Political Science. Idealism gave way to empiricism. Normative considerations were rejected. Earlier the study of state was considered to be of utmost importance in the field of Political Science but now it became insignificant. Empirical political science laid stress on studies of election, political elites, modernisation, Political culture etc." (Datta, 1989) More focus was now laid on the practical application of Political skills which are necessary for Political engagement and participation. Behaviouralism captivated Indian political science.

Political Science as a School Subject

As a school subject for long, Political Science was termed as "Civics", and was later came to be called as Political Science. In order to understand the relation or distinction between the two we also need to throw light on the concept of "social science" and "social studies"

The term social studies was in general use, but received official sanction in the report of the 'Committee on the social studies of the national education association's commission on the reorganization of secondary education' in US (1916). The committee defined Social Studies as "those studies whose subject matter relates directly to the organization and development of human society and to man as member of social groups." In this meaning of the term, the social studies are adapted from the social sciences, in order to play a part in achieving an educational purpose or objective. Thus, social sciences are bodies of organized knowledge and thought about human affairs. Social studies (although drawing upon the social sciences for their subject matter) has, as its chief aim, the training of students as effective members of society.

Again, it was believed that social studies material is, primarily, designed for school instructional purposes. This material consists of those portions of social sciences which have been selected and adapted for use in schools. The distinction between the two is not philosophical or theoretical: it is only practical or a matter of convenience. Social Sciences are the theoretical aspect of human affairs, while social studies is the practical aspect and, it was on this basis, that a distinction was made between political science and civics.

The term "civics" is derived from the Greek word 'civis' which means a citizen. The true meaning of civis is "member of a nation state", same is the meaning of the term "civitas". In this context civics is the holistic study of activities/functions and the problems of the modern state. (Prakash, 2008)

"Civics' as a school subject had its origin in the last quarter of the 19th century in India. Like any other institution which needs a disciplinary structure for its survival in the same way Indian state created such a structure where one of the important instrument of this structure was education and in education particularly the civics. This linked to the giant project of evolution of nation state and the growth of the concept of citizenship.

Few researchers tried to establish that Civics, in the colonial context was equivalent to moral education. It was to develop the character and improve the personality of the native. It was to explain the principles of right and wrong and teach or illustrate good behaviour. The purpose of civics in colonial context was also to develop citizens who respect law and help in maintenance of public order. The idea of order was central to the vision of colonial rulers. Civics was also to change the sanitary habits of the natives. It was to develop in them a new kind of self discipline regarding cleanliness. The citizen prepared by civics was expected to have faith in and loyalty to the colonial empire.

The aim of civics has always been tied to the interest of the state, which has to produce responsible citizens. In the absence of a formal programme of citizenship education in India, we can

Civics has been given the responsibility to prepare committed and responsible citizens who are not just followers but also the leaders with a critical outlook.

In the NCF (2005) and the National focus group position paper on Social Sciences (2006) the change in nomenclature from civics to political science was suggested. It was mentioned in the paper "An analysis of the first textbook of civics, the Citizen of India, authored by Lee-Warner, shows that civics was linked to the colonial project of cultural hegemony (Jain, 1999). Emphasis on the obedience and loyalty of the citizens; the colonial ethos of order, improvement, and rationality; the discourse of the shortcomings of personality in the Indian; and creation of civil society according to the universal values of progress were the key features of the colonial civics. Whereas, political science suggests dynamism that involves the process that produces structure of dominations and their contestations by social forces. Political science imagines civil society as the sphere where more informed, receptive and responsible citizens could be produced." (National Focus Group position paper on Social Sciences, 2006). It is significant to note here that this paper fails to explain how the change in nomenclature will help in changing the text / content and pedagogy for the subject and how the methodology of the subject will have to undergo a change and how the teachers will be able to deal with it.

Ramji Dubey in his article *Nagrik Shastra ke Bachav Me - Ek Academic Behas,*(2009) has disagreed to what is written in the NCF (2005) regarding the epistemological framework of the civics as a subject. In his article, he has clearly mentioned that framers of the NCF (2005) who were in favour of changing the nomenclature of the subject Civics to Political Science were unaware of the fact that, the subject of Civics is not a creation of the British but of the Greeks. The term Civics is derived from the Greek word 'Civitas' which means 'city state'. In Hindi, the term, *Nagrik* i.e. citizen has been derived from our ancient texts in which Kautilya's, Arthashastra is of prime importance. Therefore, it is wrong to conclude that the Britishers had created the subject of civics so as to make the Indians loyal and subordinate to them. (Dubey, 2009)

Several people have debated the epistemological change of the subject of civics to Political Science and have given explanations in support of their arguments. But instead of going into the debate, here, our focus is on finding and explaining the essence and the main focus of the subject which is either called civics or Political Science.

The various education commissions which were formed from time to time, elaborated in what form the subject of Civics should be taught in schools and what should be its main focus.

In the Secondary Education Commission (1953), it was highlighted that lesson in Civics may lead to a study of the working of the Local Board or a campaign for the improvement of local sanitary conditions. The role of civics is to train citizens and develop responsibility. The commission did not recommend making civics a separate subject. In the report it was stated that, "it is psychologically preferable to present subjects centering around the study of the social environment and human relations under the comprehensive heading of "Social Studies" than to teach a number of separate subjects like History, Geography, Civics and Economics in water-tight compartments."

If the teaching of these separate subjects only imparts miscellaneous and unrelated information and does not throw any light on, or provide insight into social conditions and problems or create the desire to improve the existing state of things, their educative significance will be negligible. This whole group of studies has, therefore, to be viewed as a compact whole, whose object is to adjust the students to their social environment which includes the family, community, State and nation-so that they may be able to understand how society has come to its present form and interpret intelligently the matrix of social forces and movements in the midst of which they are living. They help the student to discover and explain how this adjustment has taken place in the past and how it is taking place today. Through them, the students should be able to acquire not only the knowledge but attitudes and values which are essential for successful group living and civic efficiency. They should endeavor to give the students not only a sense of national patriotism and an appreciation of national heritage, but also a keen and lively sense of world unity and world citizenship.

The Primary or Basic school will inculcate in all the capacity for disciplined work while the University will train leadership at the highest level in different walks of life. The special function of the Secondary school, in this context, is to train persons who will be able to assume the responsibility of leadership-in the social, political, industrial or cultural fields-in their own small groups of community or locality. This does not, of course, mean that Primary education will not throw up leaders-in fact, with the proper functioning of democracy, it is to be hoped that leadership will be increasingly drawn from the masses. But leadership in the wider sense of the word (which is not synonymous with political leadership) calls for a higher standard of education, a deeper and clearer understanding of social issues and greater technical efficiency. All these must be provided by our Secondary schools in increasing measure. The Secondary school must make itself responsible for equipping its students adequately with civic as well as vocational efficiency and the qualities of character that go with it so that they may be able to play their part worthily and competently in the improvement of national life. They should no longer emerge as helpless, shiftless individuals who do not know what to do with themselves and can only think of either crowding the colleges-which, for the majority, is a dead end, or, as a last and reluctant resort, take up some clerical or teaching job for which they have no natural inclination.

In the Kothari Commission (1964-66), it was mentioned that at the higher primary stage (classes V-VII), the study of environmental activities will lead to the study of natural and physical sciences, history, geography and civics, constructive and creative skills will provide the basis for the practice of simple arts and crafts, and the practice of healthy living will serve as the foundation for physical education. Here, the integration of the subject into social studies was to be dependent on the availability of the facilities. "Social studies may continue as an integrated course if competent teachers and the requisite facilities are available; otherwise the study of history, geography, and civics should be taken up as separate disciplines.

The syllabus of civics in the senior classes should give a picture of the United Nations and other international agencies and an objective account of their great efforts towards international cooperation and the maintenance of peace."

NPE (1986) focused on the significance of research, particularly in science and technology, and deep critical studies in social, cultural, economic and political processes and situations, carried on in institutions of higher education which make these institutions play a crucial role in national progress, self-reliance and security.

NCF (1988) and NCF (2000), stated that in the upper primary and secondary stages the subject of social sciences would be taught. NCF (1988) stated that, "Social sciences as component of general education is of critical importance in facilitating the learner's growth into a well informed and responsible citizen." Civics was taught as a part of social sciences. Social science comprised the study of history, geography, civics and the study of contemporary issues and problems.

In NCF (2000), it is mentioned that the social sciences curriculum in schools will draw its content mainly from geography, history, civics and economics. It may also include some elements of sociology. The significance of the study of social sciences is highlighted as, "it helps the learners in understanding the human environment in its totality and developing a broader perspective and an empirical, reasonable, and humane outlook. It also helps them grow into well informed and responsible citizens with necessary attributes/skills so that they could participate and contribute effectively in the process of development and nation-building.'

NCF (2005) proposed that at the upper primary stage, Social Studies will include content from history, geography, political science and economics. The nomenclature of civics changed to Political Science. It is mentioned that -in Political Science, students will be introduced to the formation and functioning of governments at local, state, and central levels and the democratic processes of. There will also be a section that will indicate a multidisciplinary approach to different social science themes.

At the secondary stage, the Social Sciences comprise history, geography, sociology, political science and economics. The focus will be on Contemporary India, and the learner will be initiated into a deeper understanding of the social and economic challenges facing the nation.

In Political Science, the focus should be on discussing the philosophical foundations that underlie the value framework of the Indian Constitution, i.e. in-depth discussion of equality, liberty, justice, fraternity, secularism, dignity, plurality, and freedom from exploitation. At higher secondary stage a separate subject of Political Science can be opted by students. (NCF, 2005)

From the analysis of the various documents on education mentioned above, it has become clear that whether being treated as a part of social sciences or being taught as a separate discipline, the focus of civics or Political Science education in India has been the preparation of responsible citizens. Also, a separate field called, "citizenship education" has gained popularity.

'Citizenship Education' intendeds to develop citizens, who not only participate in the political process of the country, but will also be proactive and responsible towards social and economic issues in society. It is either taught as a separate discipline or its elements are embedded in the curriculum of Civics or Political Science.

In our country, various education commissions and policies have stressed upon the importance of the development of responsible citizens which strongly believe in core values of citizenship, which include: democracy, social justice, equality, peace and respect. Considering the young peoples' participation in the decision making process at the National level, our former Prime Minister, Rajiv Gandhi, lowered the age for voting from 21 years to 18 years. In the 2009 general election, approximately 200 million vote (18-35 years old), with many voting for first time, participated in the formation of the central government for the next 5 years.

There are two very different kinds of citizenship education:

- The first is education intended to prepare noncitizens to become legally and socially accepted as citizens.
- Secondly, there is Citizenship education that is taught in schools, as an academic subject, similar to political sociology.

All key democratic countries namely, United States, United Kingdom, Australia, China, New Zealand, Netherland, France, Spain, Finland, Indonesia etc. have successful stories of citizenship education. South East Asian countries such as, Cambodia have demonstrated new initiatives that support youth in positive roles in their communities. In the USA, President Barack Obama has cited youth civic engagement as one of his priorities in his address to a joint session of Congress in February 2009.

John Dewey has also supported the idea of citizen preparation for successful democracy. He related democracy with education and said, "upon the educational side, we note first that the realization of the form of social life in which interests are mutually interpenetrating, and where progress, or readjustment, is an important consideration, makes a democratic community more interested than other communities have cause to be in deliberate and systematic education. The devotion of democracy to education is a familiar fact. The superficial explanation is that a government resting upon popular suffrage cannot be successful unless those who elect and who obey their governors are educated. Since a democratic society repudiates the principle of external authority, it must find a substitute in voluntary disposition and interest; these can be created only by education. But there is a deeper explanation. A Democracy is more than a form of government; it is primarily a mode of associated living, of conjoint communicated experience. The extension in space of the number of individuals who participate in an interest so that each has to refer to his own action to that of others, and to consider the action of others to give point and direction to his own, is equivalent to the breaking down of those barriers of class, race and national territory which kept men from perceiving the full import of their activity. These more numerous and more varied points of contact denote a greater diversity of stimuli to which an individual has to respond; they consequently a premium on variation in this action. They secure liberation of powers which remain suppressed as long as the incitation to action is partial, they must be in a group which in its exclusiveness shuts out many interests."

However, Ben Kisby (2009) has explicitly linked the concept of social capital with the need to introduce citizenship lessons in schools. In order to tackle, what he perceived, as a declining level of social capital in the UK and to promote greater civic involvement by citizens, Blunkett argues that the state must enable citizens to lead autonomous lives, especially through citizenship education. For Blunkett, "it is clear that weak civic engagement and an absence of social capital deprive democracy of its vitality, health and legitimacy. A fully participatory democracy depends on sustained dialogue between free and equal, socially committed citizens. The State can facilitate and provide the framework within which the greater strength of community and society can be brought to bear to support people in reaching their full potential; autonomy requires a rich and rounded education. If autonomy is dependent on education, and a fully autonomous person is also, by definition an active citizen, then there needs to be explicit education for citizenship in the school and college curriculum."

Modern, liberal citizenship is exemplified by the work of Rawls (1973) who, in his Theory of Justice, implicitly advances a pluralistic conception of citizenship, arguing that the fact of reasonable pluralism means that the state should be neutral and not promote any one particular conception of the good life. Instead, it should ensure that citizens are able, as far as possible, to choose, pursue and (potentially) revise their own conceptions of the good, primarily by protecting individual citizen rights. For Rawls then, citizenship is primarily, a status rather than a practice, or rather, the practice of Rawlsian citizenship. Rawls (1993), in Political Liberalism, states that a good citizen is not one, for example, who is committed to principles of justice based on reasons that can be shared in an overlapping consensus with others, who have different comprehensive conceptions of the good. This may be regarded as relatively thin and undemanding for those able to accept Rawls's principles of social justice.

Citizenship Education in Canada

In Canada, as elsewhere, citizenship, in this context, usually contains four elements.

1. The first is national consciousness or identity.
2. The second element of citizenship consists of political literacy.
3. The third element of citizenship consists of the observance of rights and duties.
4. The fourth element of citizenship education consists of values.

In the State of Maine (U.S)

Students must leave school as "responsible and involved citizens."

These principles state that students must become:

1. Clear and effective communicators
2. Self-directed and life-long learners
3. Creative and practical problem solvers
4. Collaborative and quality workers
5. Integrative and informed thinkers

Another recent survey of 1,500 college students indicated that, young people are reluctant to participate in public life, even though the events of September 11, 2001, might have stirred the embers of patriotism and heightened a sense of community responsibility. (Restoring the Balance between Academics and Civic Engagement in Public Schools, NCSS 2005)

Transforming the Concept of Citizenship Education in India

Citizenship and its education have passed through different stages in India. In ancient times, citizenship education was largely associated with the duties of citizens and the promotion of patriotism amongst them. Up to the medieval period, different Kings/rulers had tried their best to develop loyalty and commitment of the masses towards their rule. This was the period when Citizenship education was identified as an important tool in the hands of rulers, to make their subjects do whatever they wanted them to do. These rulers were keen on educating the people about their duties towards the ruler, without letting them envisage any responsibility of the ruler.

On the same lines, the rulers of the medieval period (post renaissance) tried their best to exploit the sentiments of the citizens in extending their empire. This expansion of the empire is known as, 'imperialism'. This was the time when colonial powers encouraged citizenship education to ensure the loyalty of citizens in the colonies, so as to strengthen their empire and this culture of promoting loyalty amongst citizens continued till sometime even after World War II. Education, in general, and social science, in particular, has been used by governments, as a tool to fulfill this objective in different countries.

In the last 20-30 years, the scenario has changed. Judicial activism, recognition of the media as the fourth constituent of the government and the spread of education has brought awareness among people across the world. Revolution in technology has made the world a 'global village'. Information and Communication Technology has, further, empowered common people to access the government's planning and policies at both, the national and international level. At the same time, the youth has become so alert and proactive that s/he has been using this technology to influence the government's decisions. Social networking sites, (be it twitter/ facebook) have been largely used to comment or react on any matter of interest at the national and international levels.

The youth is coming of age in a digital era and is learning and exercising citizenship fundamentally in different ways, as compared to previous generations. In India, we have witnessed a series of events which were influenced by SMSs or social networking sites. Anna Hazare's movement against corruption, which demanded the Jan Lokpal Bill, had great success because of technology, which worked as a pressure group and acquired wide support from various parts within and outside the country. In matters of national interest and political and social decorum, whenever the Government of India had tried to put censorship on these social networking sites, the youth have pressurized the government to withdraw any such proposal. The youth is, critically, observing events at both, the National and International levels, and is able to adapt these social networking sites as active opinion forums, and have been learning citizenship, forming a generational consciousness, and actively engaging in politics in the digital age. In a few recent revolutions, we all have witnessed the power of the youth in Egypt, Libya, Yemen, North America and various parts of Europe, North Africa and so on. All these examples help us to understand that the youth wants to be a part of decision making and in influencing policy making in the interest of the common people. These are a few indicators, which suggest that Citizenship education has become more crucial. To ensure qualitative Democracy, we must empower the youth with knowledge of their rights and duties, as well as the rights and duties of the state.

How are we to bring children to the spirit of citizenship and humanity, which is postulated by democratic societies? The answer lies in the actual practice of democracy at school. It is unbelievable that at a time when democratic ideas enter into every phase of life, they should have been so little utilized as instruments of education.

—Jean Piaget

Aristotle said that people don't naturally grow to be morally excellent or practically wise. They become so, if at all, only as the result of life long personal and community efforts.

In the well-known book, 'Democratic School' Micheal W. Apple and James A. Beane (2009) have shared a few experiments from schools, where attempts were made to provide an opportunity to the students to participate in the decision making process in a democratic manner. These experiments were conducted in four different schools of the United States and the last chapter of the book, 'Lesson from Democratic Schools', presents a comprehensive picture for the experiment. It suggests that any experiment of students participating in the decision making, at the school level, requires dedicated teachers and community members who will collate to take democracy seriously.

Ralph L. Mosher, Robert A. Kenny, Jr. Andrew Garrod argued in their book, 'Preparing for Citizenship' that there are three compelling reasons to enable students to have a direct experience of democracy and be an integral part of their schooling, they are:

1. Students are most likely to understand the value of democracy-and develop the political skills required for effective democratic citizenship, if they have the first-hand experience of participating in democratic self-governance.

2. Democratic education is a powerful stimulus for full human development, including cognitive, ego, social, political, and moral development.
3. Democratic school governance offers the most practical, effective means of improving the school's moral culture, the operative moral norms that shape the behavior of the school's members.

In traditional schools, students are given information on their interpretation and understanding about their role in a democratic setup. They don't get the opportunity of practice and participation. Some experiments shared by Mosher, Robert and Andrew Garrod, have made us appreciate that Democratic societies will face some of their greatest challenges as we enter the twenty-first century. Therefore, we must teach citizens how to live together democratically in a society that will continue to face diminishing resources and increasing diversity. The public schools in the United States, could be the critically needed social laboratories where vital democratic political skills can be learned and practiced.

Any model of Citizenship education has helped the young learners to understand the following:

1. Differences among the people should be treated as strength within the group.
2. Any such model should provide students with first hand learning opportunities in participatory democracy, including reflective components.
3. Learning in the decision making process is the learning of conflict and compromise.

Towards a more Productive Citizenship for India

In India, where we have adopted the Socialist, Secular, Democratic, Republic model of the State, the responsibility to prepare responsible and sensitive citizens lies with education.

Post the 1990s, when the Government of India had adopted the LPG (Liberalization, Privatization and Globalization) model for economic growth, the responsibility becomes even greater, as the focus from being an Indian citizen, has shifted to that of being a Global citizen.

In the recent past, youth activism has indicated active citizenship. For instance:

- The portrayal of the youth in Hindi movies such as 'Rang De Basanti'.
- Candle light vigils such as the Aarushi case, Jessica Lal murder case, the Anna Hazare movement, protest marches for Nirbhaya's gang rape case to mention a few.
- President Kalam's initiatives with young people, *Vision-2020*, Nehru Yuva Kendra, MNREGA etc.

NCERT is a national body, responsible for the preparation of school curriculum and text books. It endorses the importance of citizenship education by promoting universal values and critical understanding, as well as rational thinking, through the National Curriculum Frameworks of 2000 and 2005.

According to NCF (2005), the teaching of Social Science has the following objectives:

1. To understand the society in which they live to learn how society is structured, managed and governed, and also about the forces seeking to transform and redirect society in various ways.
2. To appreciate the values enshrined in the Indian Constitution such as justice, liberty, equality and fraternity and the unity and integrity of the nation and the building of a socialist, secular and democratic society.
3. To grow up as active, responsible, and reflective members of society.
4. To learn to respect differences of opinion, lifestyle, and cultural practices.
5. To question and examine received ideas, institutions, and practices.
6. To acquire pleasure in reading, by providing them with enjoyable reading material.
7. To undertake activities that will help them develop social and life skills and make them understand that these skills are important for social interaction.

In the world famous speech by Pandit Jawaharlal Nehru, Freedom at Midnight, he had not only signified the importance of freedom, but also highlighted the significance of responsibility interwoven in it. This speech presents a good argument to help us understand that democracy and Citizenship education are complementary to each other. In India, we need to have a curriculum for citizenship which should be enquiry based, with students making connections between their own and others' experiences, learning to think critically about society and take action for social justice. Give responsibility to young students, involve them in the decision making process, and develop leadership.

Some suggestions in this regard are mentioned below:

- Citizenship education, pedagogy and school contexts: many educationalists maintain that the schools play (and ought to play) a critical role in nurturing and even transforming democratic citizenship learning.
- Our national goal of striking unity in diversity must be realized through the approaches we follow in our educational policies, programs and practices and their implementation in our schools.
- In 1999, the Indian government took the laudable step of identifying the strategies to strengthen the Fundamental Duties of Citizens.
- As per the draft of National Youth Policy (2012) Youth and local governance, including support to state-sponsored programmes and schemes:

    a) It is important that youth are encouraged to take interest in decision-making activities at the local level and that opportunities are created to ensure their active participation in civic matters.
    b) Participation of young people will also mean that there is greater accountability of these bodies to the people
    c) Participation of young people and interventions on behalf of the community will integrate the youth with their communities and establish a bond. The youth need to be involved in monitoring the programmes at the village/ Panchayat level, which will improve quality and lower misuse and corruption.

Inculcating citizenship in a democracy draws attention to the centrality of critical thinking, which has been impressed upon us in social studies literature and in curriculum guides for long. Ian Wright, in his article, *The Centrality of Critical Thinking in Citizenship Education* (2003) says, "the task of education in a democracy is to help students learn how to deliberate with others about the nature of the public good and how to bring these goods about. Deliberation about the good will often involve conflict, it will always involve argument, and judgments about whether the predicted outcomes of acting on particular policy proposals are likely to occur, and will inevitably result in value laden conclusions. Democracy is not a machine that will go on itself, but must be consciously reproduced, one generation instructing the next in the knowledge and skills as well as the civic character and commitments required for its sustenance."

In this context, Paulo Freire said that, "multicultural citizenship education has been theorized as a transformative education reform effort that seeks to help students from diverse ethnic, racial, and cultural backgrounds; experience academic success while developing multicultural civic competence."

Also, we will be jeopardizing the future of democracy if we do not plan now to prepare our youth to take on the mantle of citizenship.

In order to understand the various dimensions of a discipline of knowledge, it becomes imperative to take into account the views and perception of those who study it. Keeping this in mind, the views of secondary school students residing in Delhi were analyzed so as to get an idea of their understanding about the discipline of Political Science.

Students' Understanding of the Subject of Political Science

Around 50 school students were made to give their responses to a questionnaire which had several questions so as to analyze the students understanding and interest in the subject.

1. The students describe Political Science as a subject which deals with the study of Political issues, the Government, People in power, Constitution, Functioning of judiciary, executive system, rights, good life, current affairs and laws. Students also explained the significance of studying Political Science in a democratic country. They were of the view that by studying Political Science, the citizens get to know about their rights and duties, about the significance of elections and voting.

   One of the students mentioned that, "awareness and self interest are the main features of a democratic country so, political science connects us and makes us aware about our political issues and we can overcome the political problems and can get rid from exploitation and intrigue."

Students also explained that Political Science teaches them about the Political happenings taking place in the world. They learn about international relations, about politics, past conflicts and by knowing all this, we can preserve peace.

2. In order to analyse their interest in the subject, students were asked to rate Political Science on the basis of their level of interest out of a list of 5 social science subjects. Majority of them rated it as their first or second preference.
3. Students were asked to give their views on the need and significance of teaching-learning of Political Science at secondary school level in a Democratic Nation.

All of them were of the view that, teaching-learning of Political Science is very significant in a democratic nation like India. They explained that we have a huge youth power so, by familiarizing school students with Political Science we can make them responsible, aware and concerned to the social issues of the country. In a democratic nation like ours, our political science plays a significant role. Through this, people get to know about their rights, what is in their favor and is good for them and how the country functions and we get to know about the significance of political participation.

Students also mentioned that teaching-learning of Political Science helps in generating awareness about constitution, functioning of judiciary, executive system, fundamental rights and what is happening around the world.

Most of the student mentioned that studying Political Science helps in upgrading their knowledge about politics, makes them more aware of the current situation, about current news, about how governance runs, rights and duties, and increases the accountability of government machinery.

Further, to increase our knowledge about our country along with other nations, there are chapters like judiciary, federalism and executive

One student quoted that, "as a student of Political Science, I know the process of governance in a better way and I know about my rights and duties."

The students also said that, "we become aware of how elections take place in a democracy. Procedure of making laws and other principles. About politics of our leaders, we are more aware than those who do not study this subject, we know about the politics of leaders and then we elect our representatives correctly. It is essential as we get to know about the policies of the country and we are aware youth."

4. Students were asked about the future prospects for students of Political Science, whether it can fetch them a good job in future. Most of them gave a positive response and said that it is a vast and wide subject and the whole administration is based on Political Science, so we can become IAS, IPS, Minister and a Political leader, Lawyer, Professor, Teacher and Journalist. There were some who think that they have limited opportunities.

5. Students were asked how do their families and friends perceive Political Science? Their responses made it clear that although the subject is gaining popularity yet, even in today's time, some people consider Political Science to be boring and of little scope.

   One of the respondents stated, "Many friends say that its boring and insignificant, science subjects are much more interesting."

   Another added, "My relatives say arts is for weak students, they think it is boring and not very fruitful from employment point of view"

   Students were asked if they found political science as an interesting subject.

   Majority of them said, "Yes, it's a very interesting and joyful subject, it includes debates, statement criticism rights etc. so individual and collective views are given priority thus it is interesting and relevant".

6. Students were asked if it is sufficient to study Political Science only with the help of the prescribed textbook/s or is it required to go beyond the textbooks. Majority of them were of the view that yes, there is a need to go beyond the textbooks, they should be taken to field visits and should be involved in various projects as practical learning is more important and depending on rote memorization is not correct. Students highlighted that linking the theory that they read in the textbook with current news is very important also debates and discussions regarding current events and issues should be held in classrooms.

7. When asked about the teaching-learning method(s) which is commonly used by their teacher, the students responded by saying that the methods which are largely adopted by their teachers are—question-answer, textbook, discussion and mass media.

8. They were also asked to mention the method(s) of teaching-learning which they prefer to be used and from the analysis it became clear that majority of the students preferred methods like - discussion, debate, excursion and project.
9. Students were asked about their involvement in activities and exercises given in their textbooks. Majority of the students said that it is only sometimes that the teacher organizes and discusses the activities mentioned in the book.
10. When asked about their indulgence in additional reading for Political Science, most of the students mentioned that yes, they do additional readings for Political Science in the form of newspapers, magazines, and internet.
11. Students also stated that in teaching-learning of political science, sources such as computer and Internet Technology, Newspapers and Cinema are being used. Examples from Net trolls, newspapers, interesting news, interesting debates, current affairs and movies are discussed in class for teaching-learning of various concepts. They explained that by using these sources they get updated with current events.
12. Students were asked whether certain co- curricular activities like celebration of important days like- Republic day, Independence day, Human rights day etc., debates and discussions on relevant political issues, mock Parliaments, rallies or Protest marches are organised by their school/ Political Science teacher. From their responses it became clear that such activities are organized by their school/ teacher.

    In the views of the students, the following should be done so as to make Political Science an interesting subject -

    Political Science should be co- related with daily life issues. Practical problems should be solved with examples and students should be motivated to search and collect information.

    Along with textbooks some additional reference books with recent incidents, events or social issues should be discussed in class. Students should be motivated to watch parliament sessions also, regular debates should be conducted.

    Political Science should be correlated with current issues also, recent examples should be given in textbooks to make the concepts clear. PPT's can be used to analyse, interpret and elaborate on various issues and topics.
13. Students were asked if their teacher gives them some kind of follow up tasks after the class. All said yes, our teacher

makes us take part in the activities described in the text as this enhances our creativity and analysing skills. They are also asked to Search for material on the internet and in the newspaper about the current issues related to the lesson being taught in class. They are given projects and presentations, search out, data collection, analysis on media and decoding cartoons and funny messages depicted in posters, and cartoon activity

14. Students were asked if their teacher involves them in the classroom activities like discussions, debates etc. or s/he gives provides them with all the information on her/his own without taking into account students' experiences and examples quoted by them. Majority of the students stated that their teacher urges them to participate in class and express their own experiences and cite examples. They are also asked to collect information from newspapers and media and if something is not clear then they discuss it in the class with their teacher and peers. This prevents the classroom form becoming teacher centric and helps in making the environment democratic.

Their Viewpoint

From the responses of the students it became clear that they understand Political Science to be a subject that deals with the study of political issues, government, people in power, constitution, functioning of judiciary, executive system, rights, good life, current affairs, laws. They are aware of the significance of studying Political Science and are of the view that it helps in development of aware and active citizens. Majority of the students whose responses were analyzed were interested in studying the subject and believe that it can help them in having better future prospects although some also mentioned that there are limited opportunities for students of Political Science. When students were asked about how their parents and friends react to their decision of taking Political Science as a main subject in school some students explained that even in today's time some people consider political science to be boring and of little scope.

This shows that several steps are required to be taken so as to make people realize the significance of the subject so that they can be encouraged to take up higher studies in the same. The curriculum setters, Schools and teachers have a major role in making the students as well as the society realize the significance of the study of a particular subject.

3

Teaching-Learning Approaches and Methods in Political Science

Teaching

In simple words, the term 'teaching' refers to the act of transmission of knowledge or a particular skill. Some people define it as an activity which leads to exchange of ideas and principles and some define it is an activity which results in learning. These definitions make the concept/ idea of teaching appears to be very simple which can easily be understood as an act of passing of knowledge or information. But the concept is not as simple as it seems and the essence of teaching lies in how we perceive it and what characterizes effective teaching.

The result of teaching is dependent on how it is carried out. It can either lead to making individuals acquire knowledge and become open to learn new things or it can lead to making their thinking and actions controlled and closed.

Effective teaching is a process which can bring out the best in the students as well as the teacher. It leads to the growth of knowledge of the taught as well as of the teacher.

Traditionally, a teacher was seen as the sole authority in the classroom who was supposed to transfer knowledge to the students and the students were to blindly follow whatever was being taught. Classrooms used to be teacher centered and student's participation in the teaching-learning process used to be minimal. This practice made the students passive recipients of knowledge who were completely dependent on the teacher and lacked the ability of critical thinking and creativity. The peril of this type of teaching set up was realized and the significance of the role of the teacher as a facilitator was taken into account.

Various educationists, teacher education institutes and education councils like the NCTE highlighted that effective teaching can be brought about when the teacher facilitates learners to realize their potentials, articulate their personal and context specific experiences in ways that are acceptable in the wider context of our nation. The teacher has to understand that the classroom should not be teacher centric but it has to be learner centric, wherein, the students are given the space to think and understand. Teacher is required to teach according to the needs of the learner taking into account the socio-cultural background of their learners.

"Learning" is acquiring knowledge or skills by means of study, experience or being taught. Effective learning can take place through active involvement and participation. When learners are actively involved by the teacher then they are able to 'construct' their meanings and ideas or in short, knowledge, in their own ways. Therefore, learning is a process of source searching, collation of ideas, reflection and analysis and internalization. This is greatly influenced by the social context from which learners come. (NCTE, 2009)

If what the teacher teaches is completely divorced from the learner's socio-cultural context then the learner is not able to relate with what is being taught and is thereby not able to understand properly. Learners recognize meanings from their socio-cultural contexts, develop attitudes, begin to understand and interpret phenomena in their own ways, based on personal experiences.

In the book, *What is worth teaching?* (2004) Krishna Kumar has highlighted the idea of teaching and the problems of the education set up. He mentioned, "There is a problem of the curriculum, its dissociation from the child's immediate social, cultural and physical milieu. In today's time, curriculum and teaching is being equated with the delivery of 'known facts'. Unless we shed these notions and accept more modern, humanist concepts of curriculum and teaching, we are going to remain stuck as teachers with impossibly large syllabus and flat textbooks to cover. The school is supposed to put an end to the stereotypical roles assigned to men and women and it should ensure that the learning for the young child is related to his/her immediate life."

Effective teaching learning can take place in a suitable classroom environment. A suitable classroom environment means that classroom with appropriate infrastructure, proper student-teacher ratio and an inclusive and democratic classroom environment.

A democratic classroom is one in which students have equal opportunity to be heard and treated respectfully and fairly. Creating a democratic classroom environment means involving students, on a regular basis and in developmentally appropriate ways, in shared decision making (on various issues like curriculum, instruction, evaluation, discipline, time schedules, etc.) that increases their responsibility to make the classroom a better place to learn. The teacher values and respects the concept of democracy and promotes its basic principles of equality, liberty and justice in the classroom. Individual differences are taken into account and the teaching-learning practices are characterized by being democratic. In such an environment, all the students belonging to diverse socio-cultural settings are able to feel equal and also learn to promote the culture of democracy.

Teaching-learning takes place with the use of certain approaches which makes the teaching learning effective.

An Approach to teach a subject is a description of how teacher goes about teaching students. It includes the various activities planned by the teacher and transactional ways or strategies that are employed by the teacher and also how the teacher deals with the students during the teaching-learning process.

In the employment of any approach, the context plays a major role. By context, it means – the time, place, socio-economic context of the learner and the teacher; and the learner's previous knowledge and experiences.

Following is the detailed description of the four major approaches to the teaching-learning of Political Science.

Approaches of Teaching-Learning Political Science

1. Inductive Approach
2. Deductive Approach
3. Constructivist Approach
4. Interdisciplinary Approach

I) Inductive Approach

The inductive approach, also referred to as the scientific approach, is a process of using observations to develop general principles about a specific subject. This approach of teaching- learning focuses on moving from particular instances to general conclusion. While adopting this approach, students are provided with concrete examples and with their help they are able to arrive at certain conclusions or principles. A lot of scope is given on thinking and reflecting and students are also able to make a linkage with their previous acquired knowledge.

This approach is student centric as teachers encourage students to observe, analyse and explain which makes the teaching-learning process more interesting. It is also observed that teaching-learning inductively helps in retaining what the students have learnt as it involves leaning by discovery. Students are able to think critically, reflect and then understand a particular concept. Inductive approach makes the students more actively involved in the teaching- learning process, rather than being simply passive recipients: they are therefore likely to be more attentive and more motivated. It is an approach which favours pattern-recognition and problem-solving abilities which suggests that it is particularly suitable for learners who like this kind of challenge. Working things out for themselves prepares students for greater self-reliance and is therefore conducive to learner autonomy.

2) Deductive Approach

The Deductive approach can be defined as a process of reaching a conclusion that is guaranteed to follow, if the evidence provided is true and the reasoning used to reach the conclusion is correct. The conclusion also must be based only on the evidence previously provided; it cannot contain new information about the subject matter.

The ancient Greek philosophers first described deductive reasoning. Others have defined it as a procedure of drawing conclusions by applying rules or principles and logically moving from a general rule or principle to a specific solution.

Deductive reasoning works from the "general" to the "specific". This is also called a "top-down" approach.

This approach of teaching-learning involves proceeding form general to particular principles or from abstract to concrete facts. The teacher provides the students with principles and generalizations and makes them verify these with the help of particular examples. Students are provided with information by the teacher, a new concept is clearly explained and then students are made to link it with their prior experiences and learning. This approach is teacher centric.

In a valid deductive argument, all of the content of the conclusion is present, at least implicitly, in the premises. If the premises are true, the conclusion must be true. Valid deduction is necessarily truth preserving. If new premises are added to a valid deductive argument (and none of its premises are changed or deleted), the argument remains valid. Deductive validity is an all-or-nothing matter, validity does not come in degrees. An argument is totally valid, or it is invalid.

Teachers may use inquiry methods that emphasize deductive approaches to learning, analytical examinations of details or parts, or the solving or the problems by examining the relationship of one part to another. This linear model, moving sequentially from the specific to the general and examining objects/concepts without a context may not be the preferred approach to learning for some children from groups of color. Students of color often use a more inductive problem solving and reasoning process. They may use observed instances in context to generate an idea or a concept. They move from whole to part from the general to the specific.

Therefore, it can be said on the basis of above discussion that it is not possible to make use of these approaches in isolation with each other. In reality, both of these approaches are incomplete without the other. Both deductive and inductive sequences are valuable for teaching concepts, generalizations, processes, and skills. The teacher must decide which to select given the learning outcomes desired and the composition of the class.

3) Constructivist Approach

This approach is based on the constructivism learning theory of psychology which suggests that humans construct knowledge and meaning from their educational experiences. Piaget's theory of Constructivist learning has had wide ranging impact on learning theories and teaching methods in education and is an underlying theme of many education reform movements.

Constructivist psychology which is becoming more popular nowadays emphasizes that children construct knowledge holistically and learn more effectively when information is embedded with meaningful contexts. Resources and applications, for example, provide opportunity to them to generate knowledge.

Constructivism supports the principle of learning by experience, discovery and observing day to day life examples. This approach is learner centric. In this, knowledge and learning comes from both the teacher and the learner and emphasis is shifted from teaching to learning. Students are given enough scope to think critically and construct their own knowledge by linking it with their surroundings and experiences both inside as well as outside the classroom. Learners' surroundings and experiences become rich part of classroom processes help them in constructing new knowledge. The teacher does not provide the students with facts and information and make them memorize them without thinking but on the other hand the teacher guides them and helps them in analyzing and understanding various concepts. The teacher plays the role of a facilitator and a mentor who provides students with a lot of opportunities for knowledge construction. This approach helps the learner in acquiring problem solving skills and they become keen observers. (Constructivism as a paradigm for teaching and learning, 2004)

4) Interdisciplinary Approach

This approach aims at creating connections between traditionally discrete disciplines such as, mathematics, natural sciences, social sciences, languages, art etc. In order to explain a particular concept, examples are used from other academic disciplines as well. "The hallmark of interdisciplinary education is integration of notions and guiding principles from multiple disciplines to systematically form a more complete, and hopefully coherent, framework of analysis that offers a richer understanding of the issue under examination."(Goldsmith, 2012).

For instance if the topic of gender equality is to be taught to the students of Political science then the teacher can make use of natural sciences to explain the similarities and differences in the individuals belonging to different genders, Mathematics will be used to explain the facts and figures related to sex ratio, or the access of different genders to various facilities like education, employment, Languages can be used to explain the various literature, folklores and folktales which explain the prevalence of gender inequality in our society, and Political Sciences will be used to explain the constitutional provisions to put an end to gender discrimination. Thus, this approach will help students in making connections between various disciplines and integrating the knowledge acquired from a variety of disciplines. This approach thereby helps in making students more analytical and critical in their thinking.

Methods and Techniques of Teaching Political Science

The above mentioned approaches are supplemented by a number of methods, techniques and strategies of teaching-learning. A method is a means of procedure which a teacher follows to make learning easy and effective. It is composed of several important steps which are logically and systematically arranged by the teacher. Method is "the process of planning, guiding, sharing and evaluating learning with a group of students". It recognizes the importance of the pupil in the teaching-learning process, considers the interests of the pupils individually and co-operatively and lays stress on education as being a constant process of reorganizing and restructuring experiences. (Pathak, 2012).

In order to make the teaching-learning process more interesting, effective, meaningful and purposeful, the teacher has to make use of various kinds of methods, devices and techniques of teaching.

Which instructional method is the most suitable for a particular concept or lesson depends on a number of factors such as the learners' age and developmental level, their previously acquired knowledge, and, the subject-matter content, the objectives of the lesson, the available, time, space, teaching-learning material resources, and the available infrastructure.

There are a number of methods which are used in the teaching of Political Science. They have been classified into traditional and contemporary methods because of the assumptions and implications that are attached to them.

Traditional methods are those which were being used for teaching-learning since long. These methods are characterized as being teacher centric and the ones which do not make the learner participate actively in the teaching-learning process.

The contemporary methods on the other hand came to the fore as an improvement over the traditional methods. They actively involve and better facilitate the learner in the process of teaching-learning.

Traditional Methods of Teaching- Learning Political Science	Contemporary Methods of Teaching- Learning Political Science
• Lecture	• Case Study
• Question-Answer	• Community Resource
• Story telling	• Comparative
• Text Book	• Current events
	• Debate Method
	• Dialogue
	• Discussion
	• Dramatization
	• Empirical
	• Excursion
	• Field Research, Visits to institution of government bodies
	• Individual and Group projects
	• Mass Media
	• Observation
	• Panel discussion
	• Problem Solving
	• Reflective Enquiry
	• Report Writing
	• Source

Traditional Methods

1. Lecture Method

Lecture Method is the oldest method of teaching. In this, the teacher goes on pouring out information and the students go on listening and taking notes. This method is best suited for large classes with senior students. The students remain passive listeners; they fail to become active partners in the bipolar process of teaching and learning.

The positive features of Lecture Method is that it can be immediately repeated and modified and it gives pupils good training and experience in learning by hearing. It also saves time and energy of the pupils and is a good means of stimulating students. The teachers can add rich quotes, references, current issues, facts and debates and make the lecture both informative as well as interesting for the students.

On the other hand the demerits of Lecture Method are that it places pupils in the position of passive listeners and it cannot be used effectively by all types of teachers. Many teachers do not know how to lecture in an effective way and it may become monotonous and dull as there are very few teachers who can stimulate interest through their talks.

This method is mainly suitable for teaching complex concepts to students of senior classes. Also, to be effective, the method requires that the teacher and the learners possess both background and skill sets. Among other things, the teacher should possess mastery of his or her subject way beyond the details of the course, as well as skills of exposition and delivery-with-style. Sensitivity to how the lecture is being perceived is vital for a lecturer, and the ability to adapt a presentation "on-the-fly" to address unexpected problems is important too. The learners must come to the class with a solid foundation in course prerequisites and have the ability to concentrate for many minutes in a row. They must have the skill of effective note taking and be well organized. Other prerequisites that should be kept in mind are:

- How much material should I prepare for an hour lecture?
- How can I begin and end a lecture?
- How can I encourage students to participate?
- How can I improve my lectures to make them more interesting?
- How can I facilitate note taking?

In spite of these guidelines and advantages, the commonly observable limitations are that lectures are generally described from the instructor's point of view, and the student's need for interaction with the instructor is not addressed. In fact, lack of interaction is considered one of the major limitations of the traditional lecture. Furthermore, when students have copies of the lecture notes or a text, a significant percentage would prefer reading them rather than attending classes that offer little or no interaction.

Other key points to remember in preparing and delivering a lecture:

- The first few minutes of a lecture are important and one needs to plan them well.
- Verbal communication skills are critical. These include appropriate voice projection, avoiding fillers, using students' names, making smooth transitions, using examples and providing praise.
- Nonverbal communication skills also are very important. These include eye contact, positive facial expressions, gestures and movement.
- Effective questioning and interaction are critical to the success of the lecture. Questioning skills include planning questions in advance, asking a variety of questions, using students' names and providing positive feedback.
- The lecture should be summarized by asking for questions, asking questions and using media to review main points.

With planning and effective presentation techniques, the lecture can be a highly effective and interactive method for transferring knowledge to students. If the lecture is carefully planned, the educator will have a clear purpose of the lecture and will have considered the logistics associated with the number of students, amount of time allocated for the lecture, room size and available media. Planning will also help ensure that the educator uses a variety of approaches to introduce, deliver and summarize the lecture. Lecture notes in outline form will help the instructor give an effective presentation.

2. Story-telling Method

This method involves narrating stories to students in order to help them understand a concept. These could be real life incidents or fictional stories used to develop students imagination skills and their interest in the subject. The teacher as a storyteller is required to take into account that the story focuses on the objectives of the lesson and should be age-appropriate Stories could be picked up from epic literature such as the Panchatantra, the Mahabharata or short story books and teacher can also develop short contextual stories on the spot.

The success of this method of teaching learning is dependent on the qualities of the storyteller. The abilities to use suitable words, ideas, phrases, gestures, voice modulation, facial expressions, making use of the language that suits the cognitive level of the learners and to use appropriate aids like pictures and audio-visual to motivate pupils.

At its core, storytelling is the art of using language, vocalization, physical movement and gesture to reveal the elements and images of a story to a specific, live audience. A central, unique aspect of storytelling is its reliance on the audience to develop specific visual imagery and detail to complete and co-create the story. Most dictionaries define a story as a narrative account of a real or imagined event or events. Through stories we explain how things are, why they are, our role and purpose. Stories are the building blocks of knowledge, the foundation of memory and learning. Stories connect us with our humanness, links past, present and future by teaching us to anticipate the possible consequences of our actions.

It is a live, person-to-person, oral and physical presentation of a story to an audience. "Telling" involves direct contact between teller and listener. It mandates the direct presentation of the story by the teller. The teller's role is to prepare and present the necessary language, vocalization, and physicality to effectively and efficiently communicate the images of a story. The listener's role is to actively create the vivid, multi-sensory images, actions, characters, and events—the reality—of the story in their mind based on the performance by the teller, and on their past experiences, beliefs, and understandings. The completed story happens in the mind of the listener, unique and personal for each individual.

The other features associated with story-telling are:

- *Storytelling is an interactive performance art form*: Direct interaction between the teller and audience is an essential element of the storytelling experience. An audience responds to the teller's words and actions. The teller uses this generally non-verbal feedback to immediately, spontaneously, and improvisationally adjust the tones, wording, and pace of the story to better meet the needs of the audience.
- *Storytelling is, by design, a co-creative process*: Storytelling audiences do not passively receive a story from the teller, as a viewer receives and records the content of a television program or motion picture. The teller provides no visual images, no stage set, and generally, no costumes related to story characters or historic period. Listeners create these images based on the performer's telling and on their own experiences and beliefs.

- *Storytelling is, by its nature, personal, interpretive, and uniquely human*: Storytelling passes on the essence of who we are. Stories are a prime vehicle for assessing and interpreting events, experiences, and concepts from minor moments of daily life to the grand nature of the human condition. It is an intrinsic and basic form of human communication. More than any other form of communication, the telling of stories in an integral and essential part of the human experience.
- *Storytelling is a process, a medium for sharing, interpreting, offering the content and meaning of a story to an audience*: Because storytelling is spontaneous and experiential and thus, a dynamic interaction between teller and listener, it is far more difficult to describe than is the script and camera directions of a movie, or the lines and stage direction notes of a play. Storytelling emerges from the interaction and cooperative, coordinated efforts of teller and audience.

Besides these features, there are a number of useful tips that should be kept in mind, in order to succeed in the art of storytelling. They are as follows:

With regards to the **atmosphere**, one should—

- Have a definite place
- Have sufficient time
- Have listeners seated comfortably in front
- Not allow questions or interruptions during the story
- Look directly at the children as you tell the story

Similarly with regards to **voice**, one should—

- Speak simply, quietly and directly
- Use sufficient volume to be heard easily
- Be careful with enunciation
- Use low, pleasing tone quality

As far as **expressions** are concerned, one should—

- Know what one wants to say
- Express what one feels
- Think what one means
- Be natural

Timing is another important criterion, one should know when to—

- Pause
- Change the speed
- Change the pitch
- Vary the emphasis
- Build up to the climax

If the aforementioned essential prerequisites are fulfilled, storytelling can turn out to be a fruitful exercise that will not only facilitate the teaching learning process but will also make the class lively and informative. This method is most suitable for elementary classes as it is helpful in drawing the interest of small children.

3. Question-Answer Method

Question- Answer method involves explaining a concept to students by making them give answers to a set of questions. This method is based on the principle that effective learning can take place when students are actively involved in the teaching-learning process and are made to think, reflect and then speak. Questions can be asked at the beginning of the lesson to check the previously acquired knowledge of the learners, in between the lesson to discuss a concept and at the end of the lesson to recapitulate. They can be short answer type where students can answer orally during the teaching-learning processor long answer type for which some time can be allotted to students to answer that question individually or in a group.

This method proves to be fruitful for the teachers in a way that my employing it they can also get an idea whether students are able to understand what is being taught and to also find out their doubts which can be clarified later.

Some of the questions which are to be asked require pre-planning by the teacher. The teacher has to keep in mind that the questions are appropriate and are linked with the topic being taught. Teachers should keep in mind that the questions that are asked in the class should motivate the students and increase their level of curiosity but should also not divert the students and make them explore the details which are not connected with the topic.

Employment of this method in teaching-learning process is a little time consuming but effective. It helps students to hone their communication skills and gives them the opportunity to get an idea of diverse perspectives, students are able to become more vigilant and attentive. This helps students to become active and interested in the teaching-learning process which thereby helps in improving their learning outcomes. The responses which the students give also become an integral part of the knowledge being constructed in the classroom.

4. Textbook Method

Textbook method is basically the use of textbooks for teaching-learning. The teacher makes use of the subject matter which is systematically presented in the text book. It is important to note here that the textbook should be used as one of the teaching resources or teaching-learning material. The students and teachers should get an idea of the concept that is presented in the book and also work on the exercises included in the text. It is often seen that some teachers make use of textbook for dictating things and students keep taking notes without understanding. This practice should be discouraged as it makes the teacher as well as the student dependent on the textbook. They become passive recipients of knowledge and are not able to understand things with clarity.

Some Suggestions on the use of Social Science textbook:

- Textbook should be seen as a basic minimum reading for students and a guideline for the Teacher especially with regard to the depth and length of the content being taught at a specific class level.
- A Teachers group suggested that the text books should be free from any kind of ideological bias and they should provide ample scope and opportunity for gender sensitization and help in breaking gender stereotypes. All the sections of the society must be represented in the content of the book with no demeaning of any group of the society. The language of the book should be carefully chosen so that it is understandable and comprehensible for the students. Pictures and cartoons can be accommodated to enhance the content and for making it more effective. The examples provided in the book should be drawn from the day-to-day experiences of the students so that they can easily relate to those and understand them.

- The Textbook use strong frame to control the pedagogy of the classroom. In such a system, both teachers and students are denied the freedom to express their experiences and to critically locate their lives in the existing social milieu.
- NCF 2005 said, "Text Book should not be considered as the sole agent of learning. It should be an opening for further inquiry and therefore need to be stimulating enough for both, teachers and Students."

Textbooks must help children to build concrete and living images of the concepts being discussed. This can be done through imaginative accounts with human characters, through case studies, role play and by drawing analogies from the lived experience of the child. The textbook and the teacher cannot hurriedly offer conclusions, but must allow children to think, to relate with their experiences and debate with each other to arrive at a reasoned opinion. This had been strongly emphasized by the Yashpal Committee Report 'Learning without Burden' (MHRD, 1993). Following the National Policy on Education 1986, the Government had set up an Advisory Committee (chaired by Professor Yashpal) in 1992 that gave a detailed report on the status of school curricula and textbooks. The Report highlighted how learning can be made more meaningful and textbooks more child-centered. In the report it is elaborated how teachers are making students dependent on textbooks and guidebooks which are becoming a major hurdle in developing their thinking skills and creativity.

"Textbook as the 'Truth'- The pervasive effects of the examination system can be seen in the style and content of the textbooks... Barring exceptions, our textbooks appear to have been written primarily to convey information or 'facts', rather than to make children think and explore (p. 7). Textbooks and guidebooks form a tight nexus. In some parts of the country children are compelled to buy the guidebook (or 'key') along with the textbook. The economic and business aspects of this pairing apart, the academic function of the textbook has become dubious indeed. It is not perceived as one of the resources for learning about a subject but as the only authoritative resource. Teachers see it as a body of 'truths' which children must learn by heart. This perception and urge to 'cover' the chapters of the prescribed textbook turn all knowledge into a load to be borne by the child's memory. The distance between the child's everyday life and the content of the textbook further accentuates the transformation of knowledge into a load (p. 8)."

Textbooks are also affected by the politics of our country. Textbooks and the debates around its content have often generated heat rather than light in politics of our country. With each successive government trying to fuse a bit of its ideological fervor into the textbooks, it really becomes the responsibility of the teacher to use the textbooks carefully without any biases and help students build their own independent perspectives. Should the books be discarded or should they be used as an instrument of the ruling government to make the young generation see the reality through its ideological lenses, remains a contested issue till date.

Stepping beyond this issue, with the constant updating of text books, new and relevant topics, ideas and methodology that get into the making of textbooks, some scholars point out teachers have a great set of resources at their fingertips. Using a topic-based syllabus as a framework, that a textbook provides, a natural stimulus for learning in a realistic context can be made possible. By starting with a topic of interest and then discussing or explaining an issue or opinion, students will find out what they want to say and whether they can say it or not.

Creativity in using course books is one of the leading teaching skills. However good the material is, you often feel the need to add your personal touch, your own ideas, which stem from your experience but may also derive from your enthusiasm in approaching the teaching profession. Anyway, it is important not to rely exclusively on what a course book offers but to try and look at it critically, trying to spot its strengths but also its weak points on which work must be done. All this helps to kill monotony given by routine.

Course books are often criticized, teachers, especially the most creative ones, find they are boring, they stifle inventiveness, they are often inappropriate for the class in front of them, they reduce the teaching/learning process to a kind of mechanical routine. It is undoubtedly true that course books are sometimes uninteresting and lacking in variety. Who has never thought that they could do much better with a reading text or a listening passage than the way the course book treated it? Added to this must be the ever-present danger that both teacher and students will get locked into the book, using its content as the only material which is taken into the classroom, always approaching a piece of teaching and learning in the way the book says it should be done. As a result, some teachers take the decision to do without course books altogether, a decision which will be of benefit to their students only if the teacher has the experience and time to provide a consistent programme of work on his/her own and if s/he has a bank of materials to back up his/her "ultimate" decision. Especially in higher classes, it is a good idea to ask for the agreement of the students and to involve them in the creation of the above-mentioned bank of materials.

So far we have been dealing with teachers adapting, adding or replacing materials because the basic idea for them is that the course book must be used step by step, in a very rigid way. But for the vast majority of teachers who do use them, course books are just collections of materials, they are a bank ready at hand. They are perfectly aware that however well they are planned, they may be inappropriate for their classes. They, therefore, approach them with a degree of healthy skepticism, which allows them not only to assess their contents carefully but also to use them judiciously for their own ends, rather than have the course book use and control them. And then students, especially young ones, often feel positive about course books. For them, the course book is reassuring. It allows them to look forward and back, giving them a chance to prepare for what's coming and review what they have done. Then over the latest years course books have displayed a lot of colorful photos and illustrations and the layout of the pages has been designed very carefully. Most students enjoy looking at the visual material in front of them and this is what makes them indispensable.

Contemporary Methods of Teaching-learning Political Science

1. Discussion Method

The main purpose of discussion is to learn and educate individuals in the process of group work which leads to "thinking collectively" and then reaching to a decision. Discussion is an important means of exchanging ideas with others and "often results in pooling opinions and joint action". Agreement is the declared purpose of a discussion. It is always organized and undertaken in a disciplined atmosphere. (Dhiman, 2008)

Discussion is essentially a group work and the teacher is required to see that it is held in a cordial atmosphere. Discussion should be promptly guided and motivated. Students should not be allowed to deviate from the main themes of the topic being discussed. No partisan feelings should be allowed to creep in. Highly controversial matters or religious discussion should be generally avoided. Formal discussions may take the form of symposium, debates, panel discussions etc. they require a lot of pre-planning.

Basic to a good discussion is a problem, which is to be clearly defined. The problem must be limited in scope so that it can be understood by members of the group and satisfactorily dealt with in the allotted time. When used as a teaching method, discussion is not conducted for the sake of therapy but rather for the sake of pinpointing answers and solutions. As the group approaches the problem at hand, the members seek to analyze the issues involved in the light of evidence. Possible solutions may be presented by the members of the group as they weigh and consider ideas and viewpoints. Through this process a line of reasoning or logical thought should emerge and lead to one or more solutions to the problem.

These solutions are then examined to determine their validity and implications. The teacher should remember that discussion is not debate. It is not the purpose of the class to "win" an argument or to establish one way of thinking. Teacher and students are engaged in a cooperative effort to construct knowledge rather than criticizing the differing perspectives. Teaching by discussion utilizes one of the best principles of the learning process, namely, the involvement of students in active participation in the learning experience. A good discussion will help students express themselves verbally, crystallize their thinking in conjunction with the thinking of their peers, and develop a tolerance for those with whom they may disagree.

Teaching by discussion is a motivational technique, which encourages a student to think through concepts, which have been hazy. Wrong conclusions may be corrected through the influence of the group rather than the unilateral actions of the teacher. Problem-solving techniques are learned which can be applied not only in the search for knowledge, but in all aspects of life. Creative thinking may also be stimulated. A discussion setting also provides an atmosphere which can enhance group rapport. The informality of the situation (when properly conducted) allows group members to sense how other people feel, and identification with the group begins to emerge. In a good discussion session, one soon learns that the questions, which have been bothering her/him, are not unique but are problems faced by many of his friends. The humanness and concern of the teacher comes through much more clearly in a discussion than it can in a lecture.

One of the essential factors in the communication process is the securing of feedback. In lecturing or storytelling the teacher is dependent upon nonverbal feedback (unless he can combine those methods with supportive dialogical techniques). In discussion, however, if the teacher is asking the right questions and soliciting genuine thought and honest expression on the part of the class, he will soon learn whether they understand the subject matter or further clarification is necessary. Good discussion questions will capture a mind that might wander to more attractive mental pastures during a monological form of teaching.

A possible drawback to teaching by discussion is the amount of time required to cover any given amount of material. It will take longer to teach the same material by the discussion method than by some other method. On the other hand, students will be learning technique as well as content, and both the retention and comprehension levels may be increased because of participation in the interaction. But discussion does take time, and the teacher who is intent on "getting over the lesson" will not be as committed to teaching by discussion as the teacher who wants to "get the lesson over."

Sometimes reticent or bashful students may be embarrassed in a discussion situation. This may be true of an entire class on occasion if that class has not had opportunity to experience dialogical teaching techniques. Teachers should be careful not to publicly humiliate a student by asking an unusually difficult question or forcing his involvement when he clearly does not wish to participate.

Rambling or wandering from the subject at hand is another common problem in many discussion situations. Here again the leadership of the teacher is essential. Sometimes teachable moments will arise, and the teacher will deliberately allow discussion to wander into a bypath that might seem profitable for learning. Generally, however, he will keep the group from being diverted.

Some teachers feel safer with the lecture method. If a teacher has only a shallow understanding of the subject or has prepared inadequately, he will be threatened by the possibility that students may ask questions he cannot answer. Many teachers are insecure in their classroom situations and find safety in a kind of teaching, which allows them to stick strictly to "the script" and avoid having to think on their feet. Most teachers fear discussion, however, because they simply do not know how to employ the techniques. But inspite of the drawbacks, I feel that discussion technique is one the best techniques to teach a subject like political science.

2. Debate as a Method of Teaching

Debate method is widely used for teaching certain topics of Political Science to a large group of people. Teachers often use the debate to effectively increase students' interest, involvement and participation during tutorial/seminar sessions. When a teacher uses the debate as a framework for learning, s/he hopes to get students to conduct comprehensive research into the topic, gather supporting evidence, engage in collaborative learning, delegate tasks, improve communication skills, and develop leadership and team-skills- all at one go. (Christudason, 1994).

A debate has been described as a form of argument that "has strict rules of conduct and quite sophisticated arguing techniques" (ACT Debating Union Inc., 1996). It must have a topic that has scope for argument, i.e. there must be at least two sides to the topic.

In the process of preparing for the debate, students get to know and understand their peers better, they are involved in delegation/sharing of tasks, researched issues, assimilated material, summarized points. This plays a role in improvement of communication skills and sharpening their ability to see issues from various perspectives. At the end of the day, a larger majority of students would have obtained a better grasp of the topic and would also have learnt a lot more both, qualitatively and quantitatively. (Christudason, 1994). This way is preferable to traditional teaching/learning methods, such as passively listening to the teachers lecture or writing an essay on a topic assigned by the teacher. It is a form of experiential learning which helps the students to remember well as they are an *active* participant in the learning process. It also hones their skills of research, public speaking, team work, critical thinking and organization. Students also accept the opinion of others they learn to tolerate criticism and to mold their ideas and thinking. One thing is to be kept in mind by the teacher and the students that during the debate, one particular individual or group should not be allowed to dominate the entire group by raising their voice or being aggressive and if this happens, then the purpose of the debate as a teaching-learning method would be completely lost and it would negatively affect the peace and discipline of the classroom.

3. Panel Discussion

Panel discussion is a means of discussing a complex issue for the understanding of which taking into account the different perspectives is required. It is a form of a discussion in which few persons carry on the conversation in front of an audience. For a particular topic various sub themes are taken into account and speakers who are expert in the knowledge of those themes are invited for the discussion. At the end of the discussion, the audience is also given a chance to participate by asking questions or getting clarifications and explaining their own view points.

An Educational Panel discussion is used in educational institutions to provide factual and conceptual knowledge and clarification of certain theories and principles.

Sometimes these are organized to find out the solutions of certain problems. (MIER, 2008)

1. To provide factual information and conceptual knowledge.
2. To generate awareness of theories and principles.
3. To provide solution for certain problems.

Members in the Panel Discussion are as follows:

1. Instructor
2. Moderator
3. Panelists
4. Audience

A Panel Discussion is designed to provide an opportunity for a group to hear several people knowledgeable about a specific issue or topic present information and discuss personal views. A panel discussion may help the audience further clarify and evaluate their positions regarding specific issues or topics being discussed and increase their understanding of the positions of others.

Importance

1. Encourages social learning
2. Higher cognitive and affective objectives are achieved
3. It is used to develop ability of logical thinking and problem solving
4. Develops capacity to respect others' ideas and feelings and ability to tolerate

4. Project Method

It is defined as that form of coordinated activity that is directed towards the learning of a significant skill or process.

Project method is based upon the ideas of the educationalist, John Dewey. The credit of developing these ideas into a method goes to William Kilpatrick. According to him 'A project is a whole hearted purposeful activity, proceeding in a social environment'

According to Stevenson, "A project is a problematic act carried to completion in its natural setting". (Pathak, 2012)

As per Dewey, children should be given education to satisfy their needs of life and the school should function like a mini society in which and through which the students would acquire education by engaging themselves in a variety of group projects. Here, nothing is forced upon children and the teacher acts only as a guide.

This method is one of the best methods of teaching Political Science. The CBSE recently acknowledged its significance and under the CCE system all classes are given project work.

While making use of the project method it is imperative that certain points are taken into account.

Firstly, the teacher should have clarity regarding the purpose that the project is going to serve. *Secondly,* it is to be taken into account whether the focus of the project would be more on mental work of the students like imagination or brainstorming or it would be on physical work and a balance has to be established between the two. *Thirdly,* while conducting the project the previous experience and knowledge of the learners is to be taken into account. The project work should also be linked with the real life experiences of the learners and the learner should be able to relate with it. *Fourthly,* one has to analyze the utility of the project so that the time, energy and resources invested in carrying out the project do not go waste and the project work is able to solve the purpose. And lastly, learners should be given some degree of autonomy and flexibility to carry out the project in the way they want it to be done. It also aims at providing learners with the freedom to choose a project of their own interest and aptitude.

In order to conduct effective project work it is important that proper planning takes place for the execution of the project. The teacher is required to collect the resources, set a time limit and check the purpose of the project and the utility that it is going to serve. The teacher has to take care while selecting the project and see to it that it is going to be age appropriate and interesting for the students. It should be designed taking into account the cooperation factor i.e. the activities should be carried out in a democratic manner so that students can cooperate with each other in carrying them out.

Once the project is completed it is also essential to evaluate it and record it so that the teacher gets to know whether it has served the purpose for which it was employed and also keep a track of the project work for future use and also to learn about its strengths and weaknesses.

Projects can be in the form of *Individual and Group Projects*.

Individual project makes a learner complete a task individually and is provided with adequate opportunity to observe and gather information on a particular topic which thereby leads to acquiring knowledge. Group Projects on the other hand help students perform certain tasks collectively and in the process they are able gather information from various resources and are also given the opportunity to learn from each other.

5. Field Research, Visits to Institution of Government Bodies

Field research and visits to institutions of real governmental bodies enable the students to learn from hands-on experiences, rather than by simply reading or hearing about something. Involvement in a real world experience makes learning more meaningful and memorable comparing to regular classroom instructional programs.

Places of historical and political significance such as museums, the parliament, State Assembly, courts and several other governmental institutions are repositories of information.

The teachers and students are required to pre plan how the field visit would be carried out and what objectives it would fulfill. Pre visit instructions are given to the students so that they can observe and do what they are supposed to do and the objectives of the visit gets fulfilled.

Depending on the place visited, students are required to take notes, conduct surveys, collect artifacts, archival records, pamphlets, models and so on.

After the field trip/visit, a discussion with the teacher and other students takes place where students are given a chance to ask questions and share their experiences.

This method can play a major role in the up gradation of the knowledge of the learners. It not only helps in providing the students with experiential learning experiences but also, this involvement in a real world experience makes learning more meaningful and memorable.

6. Problem Solving Method

The Problem solving method in simple terms can be described as a method which aims at finding a solution to a given problem. In the process of finding solution to a given problem, the learners acquire knowledge about the problem as well as the answer to the problem.

This method is based on the Gestalt theory of Problem Solving. As per Gestalt Psychologists, problem solving is a productive process. The theory of problem solving, described by Karl Duncker (1945) and Max Wertheimer (1959), states that, problem solving occurs with a flash of insight. Richard Mayer (1995) noted that insight occurs when a problem solver moves from a state of not knowing how to solve a problem to knowing how to solve a problem. During insight, problem solvers devise a way of representing the problem that enables solution. (Mayer, 2009)

In the Mentality of Apes (1915), Wolfgang Kohler (1887-1967) who was a German psychologist and phenomenologist, he was a key figure in the development of Gestalt Psychology and described a series of studies with apes in which the animals appeared to demonstrate insight in problem solving situations.

Insight learning is not the result of trial and error, responding to an environmental stimulus, or the result of observing someone else trying to solve a problem. It is a completely cognitive exercise and experience that requires the ability to visualize the problem and the solution internally. Individuals are required to do mind work and then initiate a behavioral response.

Insight learning is considered a type of learning because it results in a long-lasting change. Following the occurrence of insight, the realization of how to solve the problem can be repeated in future similar situations. (Faravani, 2016)

This method focuses on our thinking process and our analytical skills. In this method, the learner is required to solve a problem, making use of his previous knowledge. According to Dewey, 'the problem fixes the end of thought and the end controls the process of thinking' (Lexington, 1910)

The criteria for problem selection includes taking into account the age and intellectual development of the students, it should be linked to their previous knowledge and experience, it should be related to their level of interest, the problem should be relevant.

As problem solving method is characterized by using high order mental activity, critical thinking and analytical skills, it is more useful for the teaching-learning of secondary school students.

We constantly solve problems. In many cases, there is a prescribed way of doing something and we fit our view of the situation and our reactions into that way of thinking and action. At other times, we may feel that the 'rules' do not apply, or that we are facing a new problem and we must then develop our own solution. Or the rules apply but the loss will be too great or the gain too unfair. It is then that we search for an alternative way of dealing with a problem and come up with a previously unused or a novel solution. In so doing, we learn and expand our parameters. Teaching through problem solving is not always easy since, many of us were taught by remembering facts whether or not they were related to each other, whether or not we were interested in the subject, and in some instances we were taught by rote. In fact, many teachers may say that problem solving in their particular subject area is not possible, not helpful, or only possible in limited parts of the subject matter.

In order to make a fruitful use of the problem solving method the teacher has to understand and make the student understand the problem in its totality. It has to be taken into account that the problem which is presented to the student should be age appropriate and based on the level of interest and aptitude of the student. The solution of the problem must be within the reach of the learner. The learner should be motivated to solve the problem and should be provided with the proper stimulus and the environment to solve the problem in an effective manner.

Work towards the strengths of each student. It is important that each student realizes and understands the different capabilities brought by different students to a project. No capability or interest should be devalued. In a certain situation, each capability will help solve a specific problem. Collective problem solving should be emphasized over individual problem solving capabilities. Some students cannot see alternative solutions or any solution at all. When confronted with a potential solution, the student may be able to contribute knowledge from other areas thus increasing interest and adding to the solution of the problem.

7. Source Method

The source method is also characterized as one of the contemporary methods of teaching-learning process. This method is activity oriented and it requires equal involvement by both the student and the teacher.

The source with which the teacher aims at teaching in class can be primary or secondary. Primary sources include historical remains or relics, human remains, sites and buildings, pieces of art and craft, writings, paintings and letters etc.

Secondary sources include those sources which are written or compiled by those who were not present when those events were occurring or they are not directly related to the source for example, textbooks, encyclopedia, articles and journals on historical events etc.

An example in order to make the students understand legislation the primary source for this would be an act of Parliament, as notified in the government gazette which can be brought in class and discussed and deliberated upon. The source become secondary when published in some newspaper or journal. The sources can be oral, which will include a discussion of customs or traditions; they can be written as well which will include maps or act of Parliament as mentioned above. The source can also take the form of remains or relics or else can be archeological.

This method is helpful in developing curiosity and interest in the students. It also develops research skills and the ability to question. Since, the source method is a bit technical and requires a lot of pre-preparation, it is used when the teacher has sufficient time and resources to employ it.

The steps for optimum use of sources include:

- Demonstration of the source
- Observation and recording by the students
- Assign the reading
- Problem solving
- Voluntary reading
- Drawing conclusions.

The role of the teacher is crucial for she identifies and selects the relevance sources, guides the students in selecting and making the best use of the sources and finally helping them in their presentation. The advantages that the source method offers are that it supplements the textbook, facilitates conceptual clarity, aids further research and when students work in groups, they learn a lot by practically performing the tasks. The disadvantages include the difficulty in getting an original source and subjectivity of the teacher. But in spite of these limitations, it remains an effective tool that can be made use of in the present day situation.

8. Dramatization Method

The use of drama can also be very effective in the teaching-learning of Political science. It is a group activity which requires assigning different roles to students and making them prepare for their individual role in the drama. It is a team work which focuses on honing of speaking, observing and acting skills of the learner. It brings out the talent and creativity of the learner in the process of teaching learning and develops their interest in the concept which is being taught with the help of dramatization.

Dramatization has been described as a 'synthetic art', involving the purposive co-ordination and control of the delicate organs of speech and muscles of the body combined with a sense of rhythm, with a view to free and intelligent expression of emotions and ideas. (Siddiqui, 1993)

Merits of Drama

- Drama has its great social value.
- It is a co -operative enterprise and develops the qualities of co-operation and social understanding.
- There are many activities in a drama, and as such students of diverse aptitudes get chance to choose items for which they are best suited and satisfy their urges, e.g.: self-expression through the various activities of a drama.

Dramatization as a teaching-learning method helps in developing deep understanding of the content as the learners are able to explore the various dimensions of the subject matter.

They are able to think critically and develop problem solving skills. Other than this it's a great activity to promote team work and good interpersonal skills.

In order to make effective use of drama as a method of teaching learning proper planning and preparation is required as it is a time taking activity . Secondly, the script of the drama should be well prepared beforehand and should be well written keeping in mind the subject matter to be covered by the drama and the learning objectives. The full purpose of this activity is attained when the people involved in the activity are well prepared to play their role. Therefore, they should be interested and supportive to make the activity take place.

This method of teaching-learning can prove to be a great success, if these points are kept in mind while making use of the technique.

Dramatization method can prove to be fruitful in teaching various topics of Political Science such as Working of the Judiciary, Significance of Liberty and Equality, Working of Panchayats, the process of elections and many more.

9. Mass Media Method

With the rapid development in information and communication technology the wide growth of mass media has taken place. Further, with the internet revolution, the convergence of media with the advent of the Internet has radically altered the approach, philosophy and dynamics of content creation and management, be it in relation to print, radio, television, cinema or the World Wide Web. The Education sector is also widely being impacted and is benefitting with the growth and intermingling of mass media and internet technology.

The Mass Media method makes use of ICT andvarious forms of media in the teaching-learning process. They range from print media, audio- visual aids, Internet and multimedia. These are used in the exchange and growth of knowledge and information. Multimedia refers to content that uses a combination of different content forms. Multimedia includes a combination of text, audio, still images, animation, video, or interactive content forms. Audio-Visual aids or instructional materialare added devices that help the teacher to clarify, establish, correlate and coordinate accurate concepts, interpretations and appreciations and enable her/him to make learning more concrete, effective, meaningful and vivid.

Audio visual aids can be classified into—Audio, Visual and Audio-Visual.

The following table illustrates the various forms of Audio-Visual aids that can be used in a Political Science classroom.

CLASSIFICATION OF AUDIO-VISUAL AIDS

Audio	Visual	Audio-visual
1. Radio	1. Bulletin boards	1. Demonstrations
2. Sound distribution system sets	2. Chalk boards	2. Films
3. Tape& disc recordings	3. Charts, pictures, posters	3. Printed material with recorded sound
4. CD/Pen drive, MP3	4. Exhibits, Photographs	4. Sound film strips
	5. Film Strips	5. Study trips
	6. Flash cards	6. Television
	7. Flannel Boards	7. Videotapes
	8. Flip Books	
	9. Magnetic boards	
	10. Maps, Models, slides	
	11. Silent Films	
	12. Self-instructional	

Advantages of Audio-Visual Aids

- Best Motivators
- Fundamental to verbal instruction
- Clear images
- Vicarious experience
- Variety
- Freedom
- Vast Opprtunities to handle and manipulate

Limitations of Audio-Visual Aids

- Apathy of the teachers
- Indifference of students
- Ineffectiveness of the aids
- Financial hurdles

- Lack of facilities for training
- Language difficulty
- Not catering to local needs
- Improper selection of films

10. Case Study Method

Case study method is a powerful student-centered teaching strategy that can impart students with critical thinking, communication, and interpersonal skills. Having students work through complex, ambiguous, real world problems engages students with the course material, encouraging them to see it from an action perspective, rather than analyze it from a distance. Case studies are, by their nature, multidisciplinary, and allow the application of theoretical concepts...bridging the gap between theory and practice.

Working on cases requires students to research and evaluate multiple sources of data, fostering information literacy.

Case study method is also effective at developing real world, professional skills. Working on case studies requires good organizational and time management skills. Case study method increases student proficiency with written and oral communication, as well as collaboration and team-work.(Daly, 2002 as cited in Schwartz, the learning and teaching office, 2011)

11. Community Resources

Community resources are a group of services and/or assisted programme that are provided to the members of a community for free or at an affordable price. Each of these resources is made available to community members to help them become self-reliant and maintain their human rights and wellbeing. A community may comprise of a group of people who live in the same neighborhood or city, people with the same interest or background, or even organizations or communities that have something in common.

Methods of Utilizing Community Resources

There are basically two ways in which the teacher may make use of community resources. One method is to take the school to the community, the other method is to bring some portion of the community to the classroom. Taking the School to the Community can be made possible with the help of field trips, surveys, projects, camping etc. The key is connecting the curriculum to the real world, leaving the four walls of the classroom, and bringing the children out into the community to learn. For example visit to the Police Station, Bank, Post Office, Hospital, Court, etc. The second method i.e. bringing some portion of the community to the classroom involves, inviting people belonging to a community or organization to the class for interaction, activity or discussion. With community involvement, students are able to learn by experience and observation and are therefore, able to understand things with greater clarity. Making use of this method involves Planning, necessary arrangement, providing students with the relevant guidelines and rules of the place being visited beforehand.

12. Comparative Method

This method makes use of drawing out similarities and differences between various concepts in order to teach them. It can be used for teaching-learning of diverse topics like political systems, people belonging to different parts of the country or the world, different theories, incidents, policies, processes and so on. Comparing and Contrasting helps the students in developing linkages between different topics and their previously acquired knowledge also gets brushed up.

When comparisons are made use of, be it the governmental structure or in the form of achievements that a government displays, it generates a great deal of excitement and enthusiasm amongst the people. Similar is the case with students, who tend to have a better grasp and hold over facts and phenomenon if explained with the help of a comparative perspective. The traditional approaches have been criticized for being essentially descriptive and missing on the element of comparison completely. For the same reasons, the traditional approaches have been characterized as parochial. It appeared that the teachers didn't bother to study the potential systems of the far of countries either because of the language or communication barriers. But now in the era of globalization, if someone wishes to teach his/her students something that is devoid of a cross sectional or a cross-cultural analysis, it'd be static and would really be of no use.

The textbook framers in the post NCF (2005) phase were very well aware of this problem and have made a shift towards incorporating comparative approach in the successive textbooks. By doing so, not only have they got rid of ethnocentric bias but have also enhanced the horizons that are available to the children.

13. Reflective Enquiry

Reflective teaching is an inquiry approach that emphasizes on an ethic of care, a constructivist approach to teaching, and creative problem solving (Henderson, 2001 as cited in the Reflective Teaching Model, 2016). This approach aims at honing the skills of thinking and reflection of students so that they able to understand diverse views and interpretationsand make objective judgments. This helps students to question their own or another persons perspective and are able to critically analyse views and strengthen or modify their own views accordingly. Students are made to get involved in activities which trigger their thinking and reflective abilities. they are required to question and make connections with their previously acquired knowledge and the current knowledge to find out answers to the questions.

14. Report Writing

This method involves making the students think, reflect, observe, gather information through various sources and write a report on a particular topic which is followed by providing a feedback by the teacher. Report writing can also be employed in the beginning of the class in order to analyze the student's previous knowledge or it can be used after the class to test what have they learnt. This method serves two purposes; *Firstly,* it helps students to acquire knowledge, as students have to make use of various sources such as finding information in books, journals, movies, internet sources and so on or to observe directly and record what they have observed to write the report. *Secondly,* it also helps in refining the student's ability of writing and expression while compiling the report.

15. Observation Method

This involves making students observe places, people, activities or processes which are carried out in their original settings like the parliament's proceedings, the village Panchayat, the judicial system and so in. This method is based on the psychological learning theory which is learning by insight and observation. Albert Bandura, through his social learning theory elaborated that learning is a cognitive process that takes place in a social context and can occur purely through observation or direct instruction.

The knowledge acquired through observation gets retained for a long time and brings more clarity to the learners mind. They are able to see for themselves, ask questions, gather information, examine and learn. Techniques like surveys, field trips and excursions, community service projects are adopted in the observation method.

Observation can take place in two ways—

1. The class can be taken out to an observatory field or situation.
2. Observatory situation can be brought to the classroom.

There are a lot of things to be observed in a given observatory situation-it can be the architecture, environment, nature, infrastructure etc., which can be observed out of interest also but the primary focus or aim should be fulfillment of the academic objective.

To help the students to remain focused, we should give them clear instructions beforehand and must conclude the observation by conducting a post observation discussion session for example, while taking the class for Parliament visit, village Panchayat, police station, we should appraise the students with the objective of the visit and tell them clearly about what should be focus of the observation.

16. Empirical Method

This method involves making use of techniques like observation, experimentation, validation and analysis. This can be used in teaching-learning of topics or concepts such as significance of freedom and equality for the development and growth of individuals and various communitieswhich can be explained objectively using empirical techniques and tests. Empiral tests can be conducted to measure the level of physical and mental well being, happiness and creativity of the individuals living in a democratic country and enjoying freedom and equality.

The focus here is on scientifically observing facts and phenomenon and experimenting on the same. Here, one of the main problems that confront one as a social science researcher is that of subjectivity. We need experiments because they help to reduce the bias that can exist in less rigorous forms of observation. Experiments reduce the impact of bias by introducing standardized procedures, measures, and analyses. Important aspects of experimental design include standardization, randomization, between subjects versus within-subject design, and experimental bias.

The comparative advantages of experiments lie in their high degree of internal validity. No other methodology can offer the strong support for the causal inference that experiments allow. Co-relational studies, for example, do not show causation. Since, a laboratory setting allows investigators to control all aspects of the environment so that only the independent variables differ, any differences on the dependent variable can be attributed to the manipulation, and thus offer support for causal inferences.

Thus, from the detailed description of various methods of teaching-learning Political Science, we can say that there is no dearth of techniques and methods available for a Political Science teacher to make her/his teaching-learning interesting and effective.

From the data collected to find out the views of students and Political Science teachers regarding the various dimensions and pedagogy of Political Science, it was also tried to find out the method(s) which are usually adopted by the teachers and the ones which are most preferred by the teachers and the students.

When Political Science students were asked about the teaching-learning method(s) which is commonly used by their teacher, students responded that methods such as question-answer, textbook, discussion, mass media are largely adopted by their teachers.

They were also asked to mention the method(s) of teaching-learning which they prefer to be used. From the analysis, it became clear that majority of the students preferred methods like - discussion, debate, excursion and project.

On the other hand, the analysis of the data collected from the teachers revealed that most of the teachers rely on using discussion method and depending upon the availability of time and resources they also make use of mass media method and group activities and projects.

Teachers also highlighted the new innovations that are being used for the teaching-learning of Political Science in today's time. They explained the increasing use of computer aided learning, PPT, multimedia classroom, use of craftwork and theatre activities, debate and mock parliament as practical part of the subjects, organizing of political science exhibitions, social science mela, MUN, various clubs and organizing youth Parliament in schools.

UNIT PLAN AND LESSON PLAN

In order to carry out the teaching-learning process effectively by employing the various techniques and methods and taking care of the needs of the students a teacher is required to plan her/his lesson beforehand. The technique of lesson planning is being used since ages and helps the teacher as well as the students in attaining the learning objectives.

Lesson Plan: A Mean or an End

Meaning: In the words of L.B Sands a lesson plan is actually a plan of action. It includes the working of the philosophy of the teacher, her/his knowledge of philosophy, her/his information and her/his understanding of his pupil, his comprehension of the objectives of education, his knowledge of material to be taught and her/his ability to utilize effective method."

Thus, a lesson plan is simply a story of the way, according to which a teacher intends to keep his students busy during a particular period. It indicates what the teacher and his pupils are going to do in that period and also how it will be done. In this manner, a lesson plan looks more like a programmed than merely a study. It should contain headings and sub-headings, indicating different things to be used, the activities to be undertaken and the amount of knowledge and information to be imparted and learnt. It also indicated the class for which the lesson is meant, the previous knowledge upon which it is based, the content and extent of the lesson as well as the various devices to be employed during the course of the lesson.

Need and Significance of Lesson Planning

There was a time when "lesson plan" was considered to be a means of imparting information to ignorant children by an informed teacher and school was thought to be a place where such lessons were given. During the course of action only the teacher was the one, who did all the talking and wrote on the blackboard, the children were all passive, looking at the teacher and listening to her/him. It was therefore, realized by thoughtful teachers that a lesson must not merely be a means for giving out information or instruction. It should rather provide a "generous" scope for the self-activity of the pupils, directed, guided, and stimulated by the teacher. Thus, a lesson plan can be transformed from a mere narration of facts into an occasion of learning, thinking and understanding. Teacher and pupil co-operate in an adventure in which the teacher is only a guide; and her/his guidance is given only when it is essential. Therefore, a thoughtfully planned lesson is very essential for teaching-learning process.

The significance of the lesson plan lies in the fact that in the existing system of education, teachers don't use any systematic method of teaching therefore a well chalked out lesson plan taking into account the age, mental ability, context, and interests of the learners is essential for the teaching-learning process. The lesson plan can contribute to the teaching-learning process in the following ways.

1. *Achievement of definite goals and objectives*: while writing lesson notes the teacher will keep before her/him both general and specific aims of each lesson to be given by her/him. So her/his field of work will be delimited and s/he will think of ways, means and devices through which s/he can realize his aims most successfully.
2. *Prevention of Wastage*: Lesson planning prevents wastage of time and energy of both the teacher and the taught. Since the lesson is prepared beforehand, its treatment will be logical, orderly and systematic. There shall be no haphazard or thoughtless teaching, and the teacher will not beat about the bush. The main points will never be lost sight of and all efforts will be made to clarify them during the allotted period. There shall neither be needless repetition nor disunity between different steps or sections of the lesson in hand.
3. *Self-confidence on the part of the teacher*: A teacher who has planned her/his lesson wisely in relation to her/his topic and his class is definitely in a position to enter a classroom with full confidence in her/himself. Her/his lesson notes fully indicate the steps that he will take and the stages through which he will pass. S/he is thus, fully prepared to deal with all the possible difficulties that are likely to arise during the course of that particular lesson. Such a teacher is sure to achieve success.
4. *Thoroughness and effectiveness*: A good lesson is planned beforehand, keeping in view the mental capacities, habits, interests and aptitudes of the pupils to be taught. The teacher collects all the teaching aids, illustrative materials and other essential things that contribute to effective teaching. This will capture pupils' interest and make learning natural and effective.
5. *Evaluation Possible*: A good lesson planning enables the teacher to evaluate his work as the lesson proceeds. He will be fully conscious of his success and failure and will try to learn

from both, for the future. Evaluation is the most essential part of the teaching-learning process which is possible only when definite aims and objectives are kept in view. Learning experiences are given to realize those aims and tests of progress are prepared for evaluation.

Objectives in Lesson Planning

In all planning, the dominant place is to be occupied by the objectives the teacher must bear in mind that there is a variety of objectives among which there must be no contradictions. The difficulty level of the objectives extends from the general and proceeds to the specific. It includes:

1. The general objectives of the educational process
2. The subject or course objectives
3. The unit, or large –topic, objectives
4. The specific teaching objectives for the daily lesson plan

1. *General Objectives*: More or less agreement prevails in regard to the general objectives of the educative process. Educators have stated them in different forms, but the substance of all is much the same. Ever since the commission on the reorganization of Secondary Education gave its report on the "Cardinal principles of Secondary education," many others have issued statements of general objectives. The teacher must formulate all his/her objectives in harmony with these general principles. S/he must be careful that the specific teaching aims s/he sets up are not in disagreement with the general objectives.
2. *Subject Objectives*: The subject, or course objectives consist in the contribution that the particular subject, or course, makes to the general objectives of education. This is of vital concern to the teacher. S/he needs to find out why s/he is teaching Political Science, for example and why a particular course in Political Science. With the general goals of education in mind, the teacher may ask himself/herself at the close of the session, 'what advancement her/his pupils have made towards these goals by taking the course'?Ifno advancements have been made, the teacher has failed in her/his task.
3. *Unit or Topic Objectives:* With the Unit, or large- topic objectives, the teacher is more vitally concerned, because it is s/he who must formulate the objectives for the units of subject matter.

The teacher must know his purpose in teaching the unit. S/he must see that his/her purpose is in harmony with the objectives of her/his subject. The objectives of each division of the course are important, as it governs the material that will go into the division.

4. *The specific objectives of the daily lesson plan*: The specific teaching objectives concern what the teacher expects to achieve during the class hour. S/he should have a definite end in view as to what s/he expects to accomplish each day. For example, s/he may set up the objectives to help the pupils understand the chief causes of the First World War. All his efforts are then directed to realize this goal- the causes of the First World War. As with all the other objectives, the specific teaching purpose must be in harmony with the hierarchy of objectives. Especially, must it be in harmony with the Unit, or topic aim.

Types of Planning

a) Daily Lesson Planning

b) Unit Planning

a) **Daily Lesson Planning**-A daily lesson planning is a plan showing the teaching points, specifications to be achieved, organization of teaching activities in detail and the actual test items to which students are exposed.
It is mainly confined to one period. In daily lesson planning the content is presented in the form of teaching points and is serialized in a psychological and logical sequence. In this kind of lesson plan the learning activities are shown in detail. Daily lesson plans should be made in the context of the overall unit plan and should be continuous from one day to the next. Daily lesson plan should not be fragmentary.

b) **Unit Planning**-A unit plan may be defined as a large subdivision of the subject matter wherein a principle or a topic or a theme is at the centre of the well organized matter. The planning for a unit is known as a unit plan. While planning for a unit, the following factors should be borne in mind:

1. *Content analysis*-In unit planning, emphasis is placed on analysing its content with regard to its concepts, facts, situations, processes, generalizations, conclusions, principles,

laws, relationships etc. This analysis helps the teacher to have a thorough knowledge of the subject matter. It would help her/him to teach with full awareness of the depth of the subject matter. The teacher will not be likely to miss any point while teaching the subject.

2. *Objectives with specifications*-The second step is to find out the objectives with specifications that can be realized through the analysis. The objectives should be clearly spelling out whether it is for knowledge, understanding or up gradation of the application skills. Each objective should be focusing on one or the other aspect of the sub-topic for the day.
3. *Learning objectives*- The third step is to organize those activities that will best achieve the specifications. To organize learning activities in the most befitting manner is an art as well as a science. Keeping individual differences and psychology of the pupils in view, the content and objectives and the learning activities should be planned in the unit plan.
4. *Testing procedures*-This is the fourth and the last step in the unit plan. Here the types of evaluation tools and techniques are mentioned through which the teacher gets evidence of achievement of objectives on the part of pupils.

Lesson-plan in Political Science

Lesson plan is an integral part of teaching especially for new comers in the field. Lesson Plan helps in developing teaching skill. It provides a framework to teach in a limited duration. Lesson plan helps the teacher to evolve effective style of teaching.

Steps in Lesson Planning for Political Science

- Selection of the portion of content to be taught in class.
- Analysis of the content.
- Formulation of objectives.
- Selection of appropriate teaching-learning activities including suitable teaching –learning aids.
- Psychological sequencing of the content.
- Consideration of learners preferred mode of learning.
- Deciding how feedback would be obtained.
- Optimum use of available time.

Pre-requisites of Preparing Lesson Plans in Political Science

- Thorough understanding of how children of a particular age group learn. Mastery over content.
- Clear cut idea about the objectives to be realized through a particular content.
- Skilful use of various approaches and methods of teaching including variety of teaching aids.

Purpose of Lesson Planning in Political Science

- Experimentation of theory
- To prepare for different responses that may come out in class.
- Logical and psychological ordering of content and choosing method and aids suitable to learners.
- Better understanding of teaching.
- Feedback from the supervisor.

Suggested Framework for Lesson Plan in Political Science

Lesson Plan No:

Date:	Topic:
Class:	Sub Topic:

Specific Objectives (2-3):

References (Used for Content Enrichment by the teacher, Minimum 3):

Previous knowledge test (2-3 very short questions):

Introduction of the Sub Topic (One introduction statement announcing the sub-topic for the day)

Teaching Aids (If Any, It should always be need based, relevant to the theme and appropriate to the student's level):

Strategy of Teaching (One or Two Paragraphs of actual Plan of Action in Narrative form):

Recapitulation (2-3 very short questions):

Home Assignment*:

Self-Assessment (A reflective note- how I feel after today's class, areas of improvement, suggestions :)

**Not in every lesson plan, if given, be in accordance with specific objective*

Unit Plan

A unit plan can be defined as a wider lesson plan which encompasses the planning of a wider subject matter. It is long term planning which teachers do before the beginning of the academic year or before the completion of one of the previous units. The identification of the content to be taught and the goals for learning outcomes mark the beginning of unit planning. While formulating a unit plan the teacher keeps in mind the goals of the unit, the various themes that will be covered in a unit and the need based projects and tasks for the students, which will be included in the unit.

It helps in making a teacher get a sense of direction and s/he is able to become more organized in dealing with the teaching goals which are set up for a particular time period. Unit planning required investment of a lot of time and energy of the teacher but the results which it provides are remarkable.

- Unit plan helps in formulating clear objectives and implementing them accordingly. When the objectives are clearly defined then the risk of diverging from the main goals of the class gets lessened.
- Unit planning also helps in keeping the work well paced and sticking to the time limit. This helps in saving time and in its optimum utilization.
- Unit Plan is prepared keeping in mind students interest and previous knowledge so it helps in organizing content in a manner which will be helpful in further stimulating the student's interest.

In order to check the utility and relevance of a particular unit the teacher should assess student's level of learning after the completion of a unit. This will help in improving the unit plan for future use.

A unit plan can be defined as a wider lesson plan which encompasses the planning of a wider subject matter. It is long term planning which teachers do before the beginning of the academic year or before the completion of one of the previous units. The identification of the content to be taught and the goals for learning outcomes mark the beginning of unit planning. It helps in making a teacher get a sense of direction and s/he is able to become more organized in dealing with the teaching goals which are set up for a particular time period.

- Unit plan helps in formulating clear objectives and implementing them accordingly. When the objectives are clearly defined then the risk of diverging from the main goals of the class gets lessened.
- Unit planning also helps in keeping the work well paced and sticking to the time limit. This helps in saving time and in its optimum utilization.
- Unit Plan is prepared keeping in mind students interest and previous knowledge so it helps in organizing content in a manner which will be helpful in further stimulating the student's interest.

4

Political Science and Teacher Education

Teacher education or the professional preparation of teachers has been recognized as extremely vital since the 1960s, various education commissions and committees emphasized the significance of teacher education for the betterment of school education in India. These committees and commissions set up from time to time, gave recommendations on the duration, quality as well as the structure of the various programmes of teacher education in India. For instance, the Kothari Commission (1964–66) emphasized the need for teacher education to be brought into mainstream academic life. The Chattopadhyaya Committee (1983–85) recommended that the length of training for a secondary teacher should be five years following completion of Class 12; it also suggested that colleges of science and arts introduce an Education Department to allow students to opt for teacher education. The Yashpal Committee Report (1993), *Learning Without Burden*, noted, "the emphasis in teacher education programmes should be on enabling trainees to acquire the ability for self-learning and independent thinking."

The National Council for Teacher Education as a statutory body which came into existence in pursuance of the National Council for Teacher Education Act, 1993 (No. 73 of 1993) on the 17th August, 1995 was set up with the main objective "to achieve planned and coordinated development of the teacher education system throughout the country, the regulation and proper maintenance of Norms and Standards in the teacher education system and for matters connected therewith." The mandate given to the NCTE is very broad and covers the whole gamut of teacher education programmes including research and training of persons for equipping them to teach at pre-primary, primary, secondary and senior secondary stages in schools, and non-formal education, part-time education, adult education and distance (correspondence) education courses.

So from time to time, various suggestions have been made and steps have been taken to mold the programs of teacher education as per the changing times and needs. Since a very long time the B.Ed. has been a post-graduation course for a duration of one year but recently i.e. in the year 2014, the NCTE came up with the Gazette notification which has recommended to change the duration of the course to 2 years and has come up with a fixed curriculum to be followed for B.Ed. Program at national level.

Recommendations for expanding the duration of B.Ed Program were being given from time to time. In the NCFTE 2010 document it is stated that, "it is desirable within a finite time frame that the existing one-year second Bachelor's (B.Ed.) degree programme is structurally transformed to a two year one, with deeper and more protracted engagement with school-based experience and reflective and critical engagement with theory". This would provide enough time and opportunity for self study, reflection and involvement, engagement with teachers, school, classroom and pedagogic activity and rigorous theoretical study. Any compromise on the duration of the initial education of teachers, for whatever reason, adversely affects the quality of teacher and teaching in schools.

The Justice Verma Commission (2012) scrutinized the quality of teacher education in our country and recommended that teacher education should be a part of the higher education system. In the commission's report it is stated that "The duration of programme of teacher education needs to be enhanced, in keeping with the recommendations of the Education Commission (1964-66), the implementation of which is long overdue."

In the Gazette document of the NCTE 2014, it is mentioned that the duration of the B.Ed programme shall be of two academic years, which can be completed in a maximum of three years from the date of admission to the programme. (The Gazette of India, Part- 3, section 4, 2014).

The 2-Year B.Ed Programme is not free from flaws and its complete success is not yet achieved because of the following issues:

1. Two-year B.Ed. Programme has no research inputs for the shift from 1 year B.Ed. Programme.

2. Two-year programme has not attempted to study the needs and realities at ground level, which has resulted into large scale unrest and vacant seats in Education colleges and institutes across the country.
3. Two-year programme has failed to engage students constructively, resulted into large number of drop-outs in first few months of the academic year of several B.Ed institutions.
4. In the two-year programme, No serious attempts had been made to strengthen the theory courses, these have been given new names/more or less all old courses with double time frame, resulted into unrest and lethargic academic calendar and time-tables, especially if we see curriculum for the second year.
5. School Internship component of the two years programme has proven to be a tool to exploit the pre-service teachers, as there is no provision of any stipend, the way it has been offered to the interns in most of other professional courses.
6. India is a prominent developing country with 60 per cent youth population and we do not have any right to take another valuable year of their life for a programme which can easily be completed in one year. This is merely leading to wastage of human resource as well as physical resource. To inspire, motivate and to attract talented youth to the profession of teaching, we must review and redefine the two year B.Ed model and make it more relevant for the students in the light of the optimum utilization of national resources including young people's time.

There have been certain lacunas in the teacher education programmes which have affected the quality of teacher education and of teachers in our country. The NCF (2005) has highlighted how, "teacher education programmes today train teachers to adjust to a system in which education is seen as the transmission of information, attempts at curricular reform have not been adequately supported by the teacher education and the large-scale recruitment of Para-teachers has diluted the identity of the teacher as a professional. Existing teacher education programmes neither accommodate the emerging ideas in context and pedagogy nor address the issue of linkages between school and society. There is little space for engagement with innovative educational experiments."

It is high time to make the teachers realize that knowledge should not be treated as 'given' i.e., embedded in the curriculum, syllabi and textbook but it has to be generated by being critical and reflective. Teachers have to question and encourage their students to question what is there in the textbooks and what is being taught in the class. Critical thinking, command over the teaching subject and language proficiency of the teacher needs to be enhanced.

Teacher education institutes should aim at preparing teachers who are sensitive to the emerging demands from the school system. Teachers have to play the role of facilitators who can help students to discover their talents, realize their physical and intellectual potentialities to the fullest, and to develop character and desirable social and human values to function as responsible citizens; and active member of a group of persons who makes a conscious effort for curricular renewal so that it is relevant to changing societal needs and the personal needs of learners. (NCF, 2005)

The performance and the output of learners is hugely impacted by the teaching-learning that takes place in the school so, the teacher ought to realize the significant role that s/he plays in the life of a child and should take the responsibility of being a transformative intellectual.

It is important for the teacher to mold the learner into an individual who is not a passive recipient of information but who is herself/himself an active constructor of knowledge. The teacher should encourage creativity, spirit of enquiry, a sense of art and aesthetics, spirit of inclusion, critical thinking and reflection.

In order to make the teachers achieve these aims it is significant that both, in-Service as well as pre-service education of teachers is carried out in a manner that they understand their position and significant role in the growth of the society. In the NCF (2005), the significance of In-service education is highlighted and its elaborated how in-service education can play a significant role in the professional growth of teachers and function as an agent for change in school-related practices. It helps teachers gain confidence by engaging with their practices and reaffirming their experiences. It provides opportunities to engage with other teachers professionally and to update knowledge. The Education Commission (1964–66) recommended that in-service education for teachers should be organized by universities and teacher organizations to enable every teacher to receive two or three months of in-service education once in five years; that such programmes should be based on research inputs; that training institutions should work on a 12-month basis and organize programmes like refresher courses, seminars, workshops and summer institutes. The Report of the National Commission on Teachers (1983–85) mooted the idea of Teachers' Centres that could serve as meeting places, where talent could be pooled and teaching experiences shared. It suggested that teachers could go to centers of learning on study leave. The NPE (1986) linked in-service and pre-service teacher education on a continuum.

Although various steps are being taken to improve the quality of teacher education but even in today's time, it is seen that pre- service and in-service education is not being carried out properly. For pre-service education, several teacher education colleges lack the basic resources to carry out the course. They lack proper infrastructure and staff. They are set up even in 200 yards land, rented building floors and even in tents, which makes it impossible to run the course effectively.

If we talk of in-service education we see that, being overburdened with administrative responsibilities, teachers find it to be a waste to attend seminars, workshops, conferences etc. They attend such programs half-heartedly and the result is mere wastage of time and energy and no output for the professional development of teachers.

During the last 6-7 years, Delhi government has organized such programmes for a group of 350-500 teachers where these programmes have come out to be complete failures. The resource persons failed to manage such a big crowd. The participants took such a programme as not more than a platform to socialize and interact with their fellow teachers, instead of gaining something out of it like content enrichment, learning new teaching techniques. The organizers failed in installing PPT systems, PA system turned out to be a center of corruption and wastage of resources. It has not contributed to quality improvement of teachers in any way.

In order to make in-service as well as pre-service education of teachers a success it is imperative that the state and the policy makers take into account the issues of teachers and teacher education in our country very seriously. The RTE act makes it clear that adequate emphasis should be given on both in-service and pre-service teacher education. For pre-service training, the National Council of Teacher Education (NCTE), a statutory body of the Central Government, is responsible for planned and coordinated development of teacher education in the country. The NCTE lays down norms and standards for various teacher education courses, minimum qualifications for teacher educators, course and content and duration and minimum qualification for entry of student-teachers for the various courses. It also grants recognition to institutions (government, government-aided and self-financing) interested in undertaking such courses and has in-built mechanism to regulate and monitor their standards and quality.

For in-service training, the country has a large network of government-owned teacher training institutions (TTIs), which provide in-service training to the school teachers. The spread of these TTIs is both vertical and horizontal. At the national level, the National Council of Educational Research and Training (NCERT), along with its six Regional Institutes of Education (REIs) prepares a host of modules for various teacher training courses and also undertakes specific programmes for training of teachers and teacher educators. Institutional support is also provided by the National University on Education al Planning and Administration (NUEPA). Both NCERT and NUEPA are national level autonomous bodies. The Colleges of Teacher Education (CTEs) and Institutes for Advanced Learning in Education (IASEs) provide in-service training to secondary and senior secondary school teachers and teacher educators.

In pursuance of the recommendations of NPE, 1986 and its Programme of Action, the State Council of Educational Research & Training (SCERT), Delhi was established as an autonomous organization on May, 27, 1988 for providing academic resource support in improving the quality of school education in Delhi. (Introduction about SCERT, 2014)

To achieve the aforesaid objective, through the tottering steps of infancy, we learnt the ropes of development of in-service/ pre-service course designs/syllabus, teacher training materials, conduct In-service Education of Teachers (INSET) Programmes/ETE Course and undertake research projects aimed at finding solutions to problems. The subsequent years saw us repeating the same processes with many variations and in varied hues, thus, enabling as to further refine our skills.

The work of SCERT and District Institution of Education and Training (DIET) covers the entire spectrum of school education.

The SCERT has focus on secondary education. The DIETs have adopted Lab Areas Approach to conduct studies, experiment new techniques, undertake action research and field testing to provide academic support at grass-root level in their respective districts in the area of Elementary Education. The inputs by SCERT and DIETs have resulted in professional growth of teachers, teacher educators, educational administrators and other educational functionaries leading to improvement in their effectiveness and efficiency.

The SCERT and DIETs have to quickly respond to the changes in content, methodology and evaluation to empower teachers and other educational functionaries to enable them to effectively address the problems of students. Along with the professional growth of the human component, the development of quality teaching-learning material and undertake research are some of the important tasks conductive for attaining the objectives of quality education and a responsive educational system. SCERT is striving hard to achieve this goal.

At present, eight Govt. DIETs one DRC is functioning under the overall guidance of SCERT. The DIETs have a mandate to conduct Pre-Service Teacher Education in the form of two year Diploma course in "Elementary Teacher Education (ETE)". The Govt. DIETs also organize INSET Programme for Primary School Teachers and Headmasters.

At the state level, the State Councils of Educational Research and Training (SCERTs), plays a major role in teacher education, it prepares modules for teacher training and conducts specialized professional development activities for teacher educators and school teachers.

At the district level, SCERT works with 8 District Institute of Education and Training (DIET) and one District Resource Centre which came into existence under the centrally sponsored scheme of MHRD for imparting two years Full time Diploma Programme in Elementary Teacher Education.

The Block Resource Centers (BRCs) and Cluster Resource Centers (CRCs) form the lowest rung of institutions in the vertical hierarchy for providing in-service training to school teachers. Apart from these, in-service training is also imparted with active role of the civil society, unaided schools and other establishments. (MHRD, 2014)

Teaching of Political Science

Political Science as a subject was not given a separate identity of an independent school subject and it remained a part of social sciences for a very long time. So, various education committees and commissions gave suggestions about teaching Political Sciences by including it under the ambit of Social Sciences.

In the National Focus Group Position Paper on Social Science (2006), it is elaborated how teaching of social sciences can help in the protection of human values, namely freedom, trust, mutual respect, respect for diversity, etc. Social Science teaching can promote children's ability to take initiative to critically reflect on social issues that have a bearing on the creative coexistence between individual good and collective good.

The significance of teaching-learning of Social Science in an interactive environment is emphasized where the learner can link classroom teaching-learning with the society at large and can understand the changes and the processes taking place in the society.

The position paper has highlighted the various techniques which can be employed by the social science teacher in the classroom so as to make teaching learning more interesting and effective. It is suggested that, "techniques like problem solving, dramatization and role play are some hither-to under explored strategies that could be employed. Teaching should utilize greater resources of audio-visual materials, including photographs, charts and maps, and replicas of archaeological and material cultures."

There is a need to make the process of teaching-learning participative where there can be a shift from mere imparting of information to debate and discussion. Teacher is required to make the students understand various concepts with the help of the lived experiences of individuals and communities. Examples from different cultures and communities should be discussed in class and students should be given enough opportunity to understand the beauty of unity in diversity of our country.

The teachers should be provided with and should make proper use of adequate reading material, it is important for the teacher to go beyond the textbooks and keep upgrading her/his knowledge base. The Political Science teacher can play a major role in making the students understand the significance of the core values of the constitution. The teacher is required to discuss with the children sensitive issues and not bring personal biases in the classroom. It is of utmost importance that the teacher keeps the classroom environment democratic, where all the students are given equal importance in the class and are given equal opportunities to explore and learn. The teacher is also required to take care of individual differences and make the classroom environment comfortable for all the students.

Growth of a Reflective Political Science Teacher

The success of an education system is critically dependent on the role played by the teachers. It is difficult to define what a 'good' or an 'ideal' teacher is but there are certain characteristics which are vital to be possessed by an able an efficient teacher.

A teacher is able to play her/his role effectively if s/he is well versed with the basic principles of education philosophy, psychology of education, and the history of their current education system. A teacher should have a strong grip over the subject knowledge. The teacher should be reflective on his/her own readings and practices in teaching. S/he must be open to new ideas, pedagogies, content area, should be looking forward to the in-service programs organized by the schools managements or the state boards. A teacher must not only be participating in these in-service programmes but also be discussing the issues, new concepts and new methods of teaching and learning Political Science.

To begin with in the first 5 years of formal school teaching a teacher should be seeking opinion and suggestions from students and be receptive and welcoming to the ideas and suggestions given by them. The professional growth of a teacher is not only about the vertical promotions in the cadre, but also about the quality engagement with the discipline and the students.

It is also important that besides the textual knowledge, teachers keep themselves updated on the recent development in their subject area and keep upgrading their own knowledge. It's imperative for them to be aware of what is going on in the society. This becomes critically vital for a Political Science teacher as, in order to do justice to their teaching, they are also supposed to give students current examples of the recent socio-political developments taking place in the world. One of the most important characteristics of a teacher is a reflective practitioner and a researcher.

The NCF (2005) also highlights the significance of being a reflective practitioner. The term reflective practitioner comes from the critical school of thought. This school defines a reflective practitioner as a person who is critically conscious and is able to employ the theory of praxis which promotes the idea of action as well as reflection. An efficient teacher is one who is able to reflect on the various dimensions of education and their role as an educator. By being a reflective practitioner they are able to know about and contribute towards the development and improvement of the curriculum, textbooks, classroom environment, students' performance and evaluation and the condition of the teachers in the society.

For the growth of a reflective teacher, teacher education plays a vital role. Be it pre-service education or in-service education, the kind of teacher education one is provided with shapes the entire personality, philosophy, ideology and the ability to play her/his role as a teacher.

In the following paragraphs, how the preparation of teacher takes place in our country in today's time is explored.

Preparation/ Teacher Education of Political Science Teacher

The NCFTE has recently extended the duration of B.Ed. programme to two years and has formulated a curriculum for pre-service teacher education programmes. In the Gazette document, it is clearly mentioned that the B.Ed. curriculum shall be designed to integrate the study of subject knowledge, human development, pedagogical knowledge and communication skills. The programme shall comprise three broad curricular areas: Perspectives in Education, Curriculum and Pedagogic studies and Engagement with the field.

The new curriculum should be such that students are encouraged to read original texts, attend seminars, write papers / involve in term paper presentations and closely engage with the field. A variety of approaches would be used for the transaction of the course, which would include discussions on reflective journals, case studies, observation of children and interactions with the community in multiple socio-cultural environments. Information and Communication Technology (ICT), gender, yoga education, and disability/inclusive education shall form an integral part of the B.Ed. curriculum. (The Gazette of India, Part - 3, Section 4, 2014)

Based on the guidelines of the NCFTE Gazette document, various B.Ed. institutes have prepared their syllabus keeping in mind that a fine balance can be made between theoretical knowledge and Practical application.

The Department Of Education, University of Delhi which was earlier offering a course of B.Ed. for the duration of 1 year. For educating the B.Ed. Political Science students, the department was following two different curriculums at the 2 levels that is, level A- for Graduate Students in Political Science and level B- for Masters in Political Science students. Following the NCFTE guidelines, the syllabus has now been re-structured and a common syllabus has been formulated for all the Political Science students without any provision to prepare Political Science teachers for Senior-Secondary classes. (*For more details refer Annexure 1*)

Views of Teachers

In order to gain an insight into the views and experiences of teachers regarding the teaching-learning of Political Science, around 10 school teachers from both government as well as private schools were made to give their responses to a questionnaire which was based on themes like:

- Meaning, Nature and Significance of Teaching Political Science at Secondary School Level
- Teaching Methodology-Textbook, Curriculum, Teaching Strategy
- Challenges faced in the Teaching-learning Process
- Suggestions for Improvement
- Follow-up Activities
- Democratic Political Science Classroom Practices

Analysis

The following is the analysis of the responses given by teachers under various themes.

Theme 1- *Meaning, Nature and Significance of Teaching Political Science at School Level*

1. Teachers were asked to define Political Science as a secondary school subject, they stated that Political Science at secondary level deals with spreading awareness and general understanding about the key terms of politics like democracy, elections, self-government etc. At senior secondary level it inculcates a deep understanding and encourages students to know about the working of country's democratic institutions and develops leadership qualities in them. They were also of the view that by studying Political Science, students get to learn about working of the government, the Constitution, rights and duties and learn how to live peacefully in a community. They also get to learn about political parties, pressure groups, interest groups, formal and informal institutions, processes, political values and behavior. And finally, Political Science plays a major role in making individuals getting acquainted with the political systems of other countries as well and also about the international relations.

2. Teachers were asked to elaborate the significance of teaching-learning of Political Science at the school level. They stated that Political Science is a very significant subject. It gives an opportunity to the students to relate the country's political system with that of what is written in theory. It enables students to become more active and responsible citizens. As we live in a diverse society, teaching-learning of Political Science helps students to understand that equality is a value and right. It provides the opportunity to build in the students a critical and informed way of looking at their contemporary world. It also helps them in understanding the significance of a unity in diversity in a multicultural society like ours.
3. Teachers were asked to explain the scope of studying Political Science and whether it is on an increase or decreasing.
   All the teachers responded that the scope of Political Science has increased in the recent years. One of them commented, "This is because as political science is not just studied to become a politician but it opens the common person's horizon to think and analyze the country's scenario and becomes an awared citizen. This is important as democracy works efficiently when voting power is exercised by an aware citizen."

   Another mentioned, "Studying Political Science can help an individual to develop an in-depth understanding of the distribution of political power. We also learn about the various ways in which different governments function and interact. Political science courses even teach us about the process of making and reinforcing rules. As a result of this comprehensive learning, one can have access to a broad range of career options and job opportunities. Students with a degree in Political Science tend to enroll in law schools to start their careers as lawyers. Following a degree in Political Sciences can give students the necessary preparation to pursue a career in the field of education. With a teaching certification and a degree in Political Science, one can try making a name in the teaching profession."

   As per the views of another teacher, "The scope of Political Science implies in its area of study. It is increasing because the bilateral and multilateral relations are changing day by day and with this the area of study is also increasing. In today's time, it is not only concerned with the knowledge of political values, institutions and processes, but it also focuses on knowledge of all the political processes and practices which are connected to human behaviour. The views of various political thinkers like Plato, Aristotle, David Easton, Cobain etc. are included in Political Science."

Theme 2- *Teaching Methodology: Textbook, Curriculum, Strategy*

4. Teachers were asked, "According to their understanding, is it sufficient to teach Political Science with the help of the prescribed textbook/s or going beyond the textbook/s is required?

   The use of textbooks as a teaching-learning resource is highlighted by the teachers and they explained that the complete reliance on Political Science textbooks is not alright and the content is not fully sufficient. Teachers have to make use of various approaches for holistic teaching-learning.

   One of them said, "I like using the mass media approach for explaining the topic briefly. If we will not use these kinds of approaches then the information or knowledge we are trying to transfer would be incomplete."

   Another said that, "According to my understanding textbook is not sufficient to teach political science. It is true that a textbook gives a direction of content and syllabus. But many a times what is written in textbook becomes contradictory with what is going on in the present scenario of country and what is going in the student's mind. For example, in textbook, only theory part is written like Indian Constitution provides equality and caste system is not practiced but what about those matrimonial advertisements which believe in caste system. Another example to show that textbook is not sufficient is that in the textbook, different rules of election commission are written which are followed by political parties but when student questions that this is not being followed in our country. Then they need to be explained beyond books that these are challenges for free and fair elections and such parties can be barred from contesting elections."

   Another teacher was of the view that a textbook should be treated as a means and not an end in itself. "I think neither teacher nor students should have the impression that a textbook constitutes a boundary. A textbook does not provide the last word on the subject. Textbook is to supplement teacher's work and not supplant it," he added. Going beyond it and making use of interdisciplinary approach is important.

In the views of another one, "Some texts should be prescribed but before this, there is a severe need to go beyond the textbook as the concepts need concrete experiences, for examples, equality, secularism, inequalities can be understood better in real life situations and not only in the prescribed text."

5. Teachers were asked to state the teaching-learning method that is used most frequently by them. From their responses it became clear that the 'discussion method' is the most commonly used method. Other than that teachers are also making use of 'mass media method', projects and group activities.
6. Teachers were asked that Political Science textbooks suggest some activities as pedagogic ways. How do they involve their students in those activities?
   Half of them stated that they conducted such activities only when they have time and resources. Some make use of these activities for assessment of the performance of students. Activities like debates, role plays are used.
7. The teachers highlighted the new innovations that are being made today for the teaching-learning of Political Science which includes—Computer aided learning, use of PPT, multimedia classroom, use of craftwork and theatre activities, debate, mock parliament as practical part of the subjects, organizing of political science exhibitions, social science mela, MUN, various clubs, youth parliament.
   One teacher commented, "When I was in school as a student, my teacher used to teach us only by textbook method. She used to sit and all the students were supposed to read the chapter one by one. But now when I am teaching, I can say that now teaching-learning process of political science has changed a lot. So many new innovations are being made for it, like Smart boards, animated movies, social science laboratory, educational trips and so on. Now, the teaching- learning process of Political Science has been changed into a two way process where each learner is an active participant of classroom activity."

8. Teachers were asked to answer to the question, can Political Science education be imparted through co-curricular/ co-scholastic activities? If yes, mention some of the activities organized in your school which lead to the promotion of learning Political Science.

While explaining the significance of co-curricular/ co-scholastic activities the teachers mentioned how they can help in teaching-learning of Political Science and what all activities are organized by them.

One of them said, "Yes we can make use of such activities, we can ask our students to explore their environment by various means like observation, survey etc. After this they work in pairs or in a group they will conclude what are the differences or similarities in their environment. Various topics like working of their respective political representatives, the MCD, condition of government hospitals and so on can be covered by this method".

Another teacher mentioned that "Yes, in fact, Political Science best fits in the category of subjects that can be effectively taught and learnt through co-curricular activities. In my school various mock activities such as village panchayat, parliament proceeding, visit to actual place and role play activities have been organized and they were really helpful...."

Another teacher commented that "Yes co-curricular activities helps a lot in imparting Political Science education. Students in school are at that age where they are full of energy and full of creativity. Asking them to read and understand will not develop any interest as this task can be done by themselves also so the role of teacher is to give them an alternative way to understand the topic." Keeping all this in mind, following activities were conducted by me:

- Paste five matrimonial advertisements each describing caste, religion as their preference and other five in which caste is not considered.
- Panchayat elections in class followed by discussion on utilization of funds for village development.
- Film screening and review, *sanvidhan* series.
- Morning assembly activities, inter house competitions, quiz competitions, play on various special assemblies and functions, selection of monitors in every class, model making.

9. The next question that was asked was, "As a teacher, what do you do to upgrade your knowledge of Political Science (At Individual level/ At Institutional level/ During In-Service Programme)?"

   Most of them stated that it's important to keep oneself updated and they do so by using various means, the popular ones are use of newspaper and journals, internet sources, reference books and attending workshops and seminars.

   One commented, "One should never consider themselves as perfect as it stops the possibility to improve and the best teacher is the one who adapts to the changing times. Considering this, I attend different workshops, seminars, read books, newspapers etc."

   Another commented, "I read books written by different writers, watch documentaries, update myself with mass media, keep in touch with subject experts, make use of library, read journals and newspapers. One of them also stated that viewing YouTube video lessons and surfing through Educational websites keep teachers updated."

Theme 3- *Challenges Faced in the Teaching-Learning Process*

10. Teachers were asked "As per your understanding, how do your students perceive Political Science? Do they find it interesting?"

    Teachers explained how their students perceive Political Science. Most of them believed that their students find it to be interesting and that the interest in a particular subject is also dependent on the way it is taught in class and on the kind of method and approach of teaching applied by the teacher.

    One of them commented most of the students think that social science subjects are very boring, especially history but when it comes to political science, students feel it is one of the interesting subject because they think they are studying what they actually see in their society.

    Another teacher commented, "Students consider political science interesting when they are able to relate with what is being taught in class. They develop interest when the subject matter comes to them in an interesting and clear manner."

Another one stated, "Initially they used to tell me that it is a boring subject but after few days of teaching I was able to evoke interest of my learners in the subject. Since they have never been taught by different methods, which could be one reason for not liking the subject initially"

"As I observed in my classes maximum students have interest in this subject, they find it interesting because election process, formation of central or state government, political parties etc. are related to their daily life situations. They find it interesting because I try to develop their interest, link it with their own experiences and previous knowledge instead of lecture method, I make use of action method/ project."

11. Teachers were asked to think and tell which teaching strategy of Political Science adopted by them develops or increases students' interest in the class?

    Commonly used strategies which most of the teachers think effective are making use of mass media, activity method—showing videos, poster making competition, inter-school debate competition, youth parliament, mock play of elections of panchayat, educational field trips to parliament, celebrating significant days like Independence day, Republic day etc.

    One commented, "Why can't we organize 'Political Science fest' and impart knowledge through interesting ways. Why can't we organize plays or drama based on the contribution of our freedom fighters and heroes instead of just Julius Caesar plays?... Through these activities students would definitely become keen to play the lead role of freedom fighters and will develop interest and understanding of our national history and will respect them also."

12. What challenges do you face while teaching Political Science in class? Is there any particular topic(s) in the prescribed syllabus which is difficult to teach?

    The challenges mainly faced by the teachers are lack of time and resources. Some teachers were of the view that sometimes the lack of sufficient previously acquired knowledge of students and lack of interest or efforts in reading newspapers and other sources acts as an impediment in teaching-learning.

One stated, "…Challenge not as such but sometimes because of time and systemic flaws we need to restrict our knowledge and explanation. There is no such difficulty in topic but while teaching topics like reservation, secularism, gender, equality etc. I need to give them full unbiased information and my information is based on facts and theories. As a teacher I don't want to make any group feel bad or neglected and discriminated on the basis of caste, colour, religion etc.

Another commented, "lack of previous knowledge, irregularity of reading newspaper and other relevant sources... becomes a hurdle for proper discussion…"

Theme 4- *Suggestions for Improvement*

13. Teachers were asked to suggest what should be done to make Political Science teaching- learning more effective?
    In the views of teachers, in order to make teaching-learning of Political Science more interesting and effective they should not consider students as passive learners because this leads to the lack of development of interest of students in the subject. They were of the view that no matter what method one is using for teaching-learning process, one should always try to engage learners in classroom activities. Innovative techniques, examples from real life situations, use of ICT and interactive teaching-learning process were quoted as being the key towards effective teaching-learning of Political Science.

    One quoted, "I plan those things which I would wish or expect from my teacher. I think about what all things or activities make the topic interesting for me? Keeping this in mind I plan activities like mock plays, debates, posters etc. and this surely helps my students in getting more interested and engaged"

    Another mentioned, "We have to change our methodology according to the students. If some of them are not able to understand the topic. We have to give them extra time with a different methodology (what they need)".

    "….use of innovative techniques, use of illustrations from real life situations, Interactive teaching-learning process, research, resources in schools, mass media and communication technology should be brought closer to the students"

Theme 5- *Follow-Up Activities*

14. Do you think it is important to give some follow-up activity to the students after class?
    Most of the teachers said that yes follow up activities are important but it is not necessary to give follow up activities after each class.
15. Teachers were asked to suggest different ways as follow-up tasks in Political Science.
    The most common follow up tasks for classes 6th, 7th includes textbook reading, quiz, open book exercises, picture analysis, collecting newspaper cuttings, discussion with family. For classes 8th to 10th the follow up tasks include report writing, small group activities, refer other books or websites for further studies and for 11th and 12th these include debate, presentation, organizing clubs based on themes, assignments, surveys

Theme 6- *Democratic Political Science Classroom*

16. In order to analyze whether the teachers believe in promoting and maintaining of a democratic classroom environment, teachers were asked if they engage in any sort of discussion with students while teaching.
    Most of the teachers believed in the significance of discussion in order to increase classroom participation and including learners own experiences and real life situations.
    One of them stated, "Yes mostly my class starts with familiarizing the topic to students and this starts with discussion. I give them the opportunity to express their views."
    Another stated, "Yes, I have engaged learners in discussions on almost all the topics that I have taught so far. The best discourses I have conducted till now were on the topics of marginalization, secularism, democracy, rights and so on."
17. Teachers were asked how they promote the values of Democracy, Secularism and Republic among their students. They highlighted the significance of taking care of individual differences, non-discrimination on any ground, encouraging all students to participate in the teaching-learning process. Making students understand the significance of democracy and rights. Promoting a secular environment in the school and class,

> celebrating various festivals and making students interested in knowing about various religions by making them involved in different activities. Also, inculcating in them the values of equality, fraternity and the significance of a democratic republic by acquainting them with the core values of our Constitution and telling them about our freedom struggle.

One quoted, "Students practice what they observe. Being a teacher, we should always preach what we teach. The best way to promote these values, a teacher should be democratic and secular in the classroom situation and other rituals in the school premises.

Considering individual differences of learners, a teacher should treat all the students in a way that no other student feel discriminated or ignored. Discussions can also play a very important role in promoting Democracy, Secularism, and Republic among students.

The value of democracy can be inculcated by highlighting the condition and necessity in which we adopted democracy. We should highlight the importance of rights enjoyed in a democratic country."

Another stated, "We can promote Secularism by emphasizing the contribution of people from all religion, to give activities like making observations and after interaction finding out different festivals, eating habits, history of different cultures, festivals and customs of diversed groups. Also, to find out contribution of people belonging to different religions, culture in the nation's development."

"For explaining the significance of Republic, students are being familiarized with the challenges faced before and after formation of Indian Constitution. Telling them some instances about the struggle and fight we made for achieving this. Real life examples will be very helpful.

Comparative study of non-democratic, non-secular and non-republic nations with India can also be conducted so as to make students understand the significance of a democratic country like ours.

Analysis

As per the views of various teachers, the subject of Political Science includes into its domain various facets of the Government and Politics and it also includes the study of views of various Political thinkers. Teachers explained that it's a subject of vast scope and of great significance.

They elaborated that the scope is on an increase these days it helps individuals in getting an in-depth knowledge about the working of the governments and how to actively take part in the governmental processes and as far as job is concerned – in today's time several avenues open up for an individual if she/he studies Political Science.

Political Science teachers also gave their views about the teaching methodology the curriculum and the strategies adopted for the teaching learning of Political Science, while explaining their views about the nature and the role of the commonly prescribed textbooks they stated that teachers should not be completely dependent on the textbooks it should be considered to be one of the teaching-learning resources and not the 'only resource'. There is a need to go beyond textbooks and make use of other significant teaching-learning resources as well. Teachers also expressed that there is a need to revise the textbooks from time to time and link them with the current socio-political situation in order to make them more comprehensive and holistic. Certain activities are mentioned in the book as pedagogic ways, they make use of activities like role plays and debates when they have ample amount of time.

As far as the teaching method is concerned, most of the teachers rely on using discussion method and depending upon the availability of time and resources they also make use of mass media method and group activities and projects.

Teachers also highlighted about the new innovations that are being used for the teaching-learning of Political Science in today's time they explained the increasing use and employment of computer aided learning, PPT, multimedia classroom, use of craftwork and theatre activities, debate, mock parliament as practical part of the subjects, organizing of Political Science exhibitions, Social Science mela, MUN, various clubs and organizing youth Parliament in schools.

They elaborated the role of co-curricular activities for the teaching-learning of Political Science. Wide range of activities can be used to increase students' interest and creativity and increase the learning outcome. Popularly used activities are individual and group projects, observation, surveys, model making, mock activities such as mock village Panchayat, setting up of mock Parliament, field visits, film screening and review, quiz, debates and depictions of socio-political issues in morning assembly.

When asked about the up gradation of the knowledge of in-service teachers, all the teachers explained that yes it is extremely important and they do so by making use of various means and the popular ones are use of newspaper and journals, internet sources, reference books and attending workshops and seminars.

Teachers were asked about how their students perceive Political Science and do they find it to be an interesting subject. Most of them believed that their students find it to be interesting and that the interest in a particular subject is also dependent on the way it is taught in class, on the method and approach being employed by the teacher.

Teachers also commented on the challenges mainly faced by the teachers while teaching Political Science in class the most common challenge mentioned by majority of them is lack of time and resources. Some teachers were of the view that sometimes the lack of sufficient previously acquired knowledge of students and lack of interest or efforts in reading newspapers and other sources acts as an impediment in teaching-learning.

In the views of teachers in order to make teaching-learning of Political Science more interesting and effective, they should not consider students as passive learners because this leads to the lack of development of interest of students in the subject. They were of the view that no matter what method one is using for teaching learning process, one should always try to engage learners in classroom activities. Innovative techniques, examples from real life situations, use of ICT and interactive teaching learning process were quoted as being the key towards effective teaching-learning of Political Science.

When asked about the use of follow up tasks most of the teachers said that yes follow up activities are important but it is not necessary to give follow up activities after each class so it depends on the topic.

The most common follow up tasks included for classes:

6th, 7th – textbook reading, quiz, open book exercises, picture analysis, collecting newspaper cuttings, discussion with family;

8th to 10th—report writing, small group activities, refer other books or websites for further studies; and

11th and 12th—debate, presentation, organizing clubs based on themes, assignments and surveys.

In order to analyze whether the teachers believe in promoting and maintaining of a democratic classroom environment, teachers were asked if they engage in any sort of discussion with students while teaching and they explained:

Most of the teachers believed in the significance of discussion in order to increase classroom participation and including learners own experiences and real life situations.

Teachers were asked how they promote the values of Democracy, Secularism and Republic in their students. They highlighted the significance of taking care of individual differences, non-discrimination on any grounds, encouraging all students to participate in the teaching-learning process. Making students understand the significance of democracy and rights. Promoting a secular environment in the school and class, celebrating various festivals, making students interested in knowing about various religions by making them involved in different activities. Also, inculcating in them the values of equality, fraternity and the significance of a democratic republic by acquainting them with the core values of our constitution, making them involved in comparative study of non-democratic, non-secular and non-republic nation with India and by telling them stories about our countries freedom struggle.

In sum, it is essential to reiterate the fact that teachers can play a vital role in the growth and development of a subject and in making individuals realize its scope and significance. In the present era several new innovative techniques of teaching-learning are coming up which are proving to be effective pedagogical tools. Both in-service and pre-service teachers are required to keep themselves updated about the new developments and should incorporate these in their teaching process. Teacher training institutes should work on improving the quality of education that is being provided to pupil teachers and schools should provide teachers with an environment where there they can respect their job and themselves. The continuous professional development of teachers should also be taken care of. The policy framers should provide teachers with platforms where they can hone their teaching and research skills.

Teachers should learn to respect the democratic principles and incorporate the same in their classrooms and with their colleagues. They are required to understand the needs of the students and what they are supposed to do to bring out the best in each student. With this approach teachers can prove to be real role models and help in the betterment of the society.

5

Critical Pedagogy, Inclusive and Democratic Classroom for Political Science

Critical Pedagogy is a philosophy of education whose oldest propagator was Paulo Freire and later Henry Giroux developed it as an educational movement. Critical Pedagogy aims at enabling students to develop consciousness of freedom, to recognize authoritarian tendencies and connect knowledge to power and the ability to take constructive action (Giroux, 2010).

It focuses on the relevance of critical thinking, self-reflection and the ability to analyze and question. It aims at transforming individuals from 'passive recipients' of knowledge to 'active constructors' who grow in a democratic environment.

Critical Pedagogy is based on the Marxist theory and its premise that the power of capitalism has come to dominate all aspects of both, social life and the means of social control in the society. The system of education is also not divorced from it and if left unchecked then education can play the role of a key factor of perpetration and continuance of injustices and evils prevalent in the society.

So, education should be transformed and should be used in such a way that it empowers individuals and groups and becomes a means of changing the social, economic, and political structures of society that support oppression.

Implications of Critical Pedagogy for Political Science

Critical pedagogues like Paulo Freire assert that education should be able to prevent the reproduction of an unjust society and its various segments. In his landmark work, *Pedagogy of the Oppressed,* Freire

(1970/2005) explained that prevailing system of education is trapped in a web which cannot let it act as a liberating force as the education itself is promoting the unequal power relations and maintain the status quo.

Freire, with the help of his work explained the lacunas that were present in the education system. He described that teachers were making use of the *banking model* of education which led to '*narration sickness.*' In other words, teachers make students blindly follow their lectures without keeping in mind students' own life experiences; treating them as passive recipients of knowledge who lack the ability to construct their own knowledge. In order to put an end to this system and raising a voice, he called for adopting the process of *conscientization*, which is the act of seeing contradictions and taking action against oppressive conditions in society (Irwin, 2012).

Freire explained that the solution to the problems of the education system and the society lies in education itself. He saw schools not as simply the reproducers of capitalist technology, but also a place where that reproduction could be challenged (Giroux, 1984)

Freire gave significance to dialogue as a means to end oppression and making people realize that there is something wrong or missing in their current situation. With the help of dialogue as a pedagogic technique, teachers can help students in being active and reflective who in turn also helps the teacher in adding more to his/her existing knowledge with the help of the students.

Other critical pedagogues like, Henry Giroux were influenced by Freire's work and drew their views on critical pedagogy from his work. Giroux highlighted the significance of Freirean dialogic technique for the promotion of democratic education.

In Giroux's own words-

> "I am drawn to Paulo Freire's (1970/2005) conception of education as a dialogue between students-teachers and teacher-student, as it challenges the asymmetrical power relationships between teacher and students. His is a vision of democratic education. Viewed through a critical lens, the classroom is a democratic public sphere dedicated to self- and social empowerment (Giroux & McLaren, 1986). Linking critical pedagogy and democratization allows people "to question what it is they have become within existing institutional and social formations, and to give some thought to what it might mean to transform existing relations of subordination and oppression" (Giroux, 2004,).

Defined in this way, the classroom becomes not a place in which knowledge is transferred from teacher to student, but a place wherein students challenge oppressive social and educational norms. (Wylie, 2014)

They recognize that classrooms are sites of struggles "waged in the name of developing a more just, humane, and equitable social order, both within and outside schools" (Giroux, 2009). Critical pedagogues aim to do more than provide students with the knowledge and skills to be productive citizens; they work with students to construct a society based upon social justice (McLaren, 2009).

Critical Pedagogues like, Pierre Bourdieu, Michael Apple and others have also explained the significance of dialogue, critique and practice. They highlighted that these core elements of critical pedagogy are more or less absent in conventional classroom settings. There is a need to overcome the conventional culture of silence so that students can gather a sense of freedom and empowerment.

Henry Giroux, in *ideology, culture and the process of schooling* explained that the pedagogy should encourage self-reflection and communicative interaction, if it fails to do so, it ends up providing students with the illusion rather than the substance of choice, promotes manipulation and it denies critical reflection. (Giroux, 1984)

So the education system and the classroom environment of a Political Science classroom should be such that enough opportunity is provided to the students to think, reflect and question what is being taught to them. They should be given the space to understand different perspectives. The teacher should teach the concepts in such a way that they don't appear to be alien to the students this can be done by relating the information being provided to students with students' socio- cultural environment and comparing and contrasting it. Learner's own experiences should be taken into account and used as example to explain a particular topic. Another significant point is to maintain a democratic classroom environment in the class; the teacher should not encourage discrimination in any form and should also take note of individual differences while teaching.

NCF (2005) has also elaborated the significance of adopting critical pedagogy of education. It is stated in the NCF (2005) that "teacher and student engagement is critical in the classroom because it has the power to define whose knowledge will become a part of school-related knowledge and whose voices will shape it. Students are not just young people for whom adults should devise solutions. They are critical observers of their own conditions and needs, and should be participants in discussions and problem solving related to their education and future opportunities. Hence children need to be aware that their experiences and perceptions are important and should be encouraged to develop the mental skills needed to think and reason independently and have the courage to dissent." (NCF, 2005)

Children should be encouraged and given the space to make connections between what they learn inside as well as outside the school. Their experiences outside the school also help in honing their capacities, learning abilities, and expanding their knowledge base which further enhances the learning process.

Critical pedagogy gives an opportunity to reflect critically on issues in terms of their social, political, economic and moral aspects. It helps individuals to widen up their perspectives and to consider a multitude of views on social issues. It promotes respect and a commitment to democratic forms of interaction. This is important in light of the multiple contexts in which our schools function.

A critical framework helps children to see social issues from different perspectives and understand how such issues are connected to their lives. For instance, understanding of democracy as a way of life can be chartered through a path where children reflect on how they regard others (e.g. friends, neighbors, the opposite sex, elders, etc.), how they make choices (e.g. activities, play, friends, career, etc.), and how they cultivate the ability to make decisions. Likewise, issues related to human rights, caste, religion and gender can be critically reflected on by children in order to see how these issues are connected to their everyday experiences, and also how different forms of inequalities become compounded and are perpetuated. Critical pedagogy facilitates collective decision making through open discussion and by encouraging and recognizing multiple views. (NCF, 2005)

In a society there are certain groups of people who are divorced from the mainstream and enjoy a different culture, language and traditions. In India some of the indigenous tribal can be grouped under this category. Steps are taken to mainstream them by giving them educational opportunities but in this process of mainstreaming, do we take care of their rich culture? Do we think about teaching them in their own language, which might or might not have a script? Do we give them enough representation in our textbooks? Does educating them come at a cost of divorcing them from their diverse culture?

Indigenous/Red Pedagogy

Sandy Grande, in her work, *Red Pedagogy: Native American Social and Political Thought* tried to find the answers to these questions. Drawing on her experience and knowledge as a Quechua woman living in the United States, she focused on the educational experiences of the indigenous people who in the name of mainstreaming are taken far away from their cultural roots. Grande elaborated that the colonized form of education has been practiced by educators for the past century in federally operated schools under the false assumption that the goal of "education" is to mould all students to become part of the mainstream. (Grande, 2015)

For protecting the culture and practices of the indigenous groups, Grande proposes undertaking a Red pedagogy which aims at accepting a 'revolutionary critical pedagogy' that encompasses valuable knowledge contained in Indigenous experience and world-views, seen as essential by Grande for transforming capitalist social relations between humankind and all of Creation.

A red pedagogy is about engaging the development of community based power in the interest of a responsible political, economic and spiritual society. One element of Red Pedagogy is its insistence that Native Americans in general, including indigenous scholars, and non-natives need to critique, challenge, and even reject dominant modes of thought that have been applied to indigenous populations for years.

As Mitchell (2001) notes," the production of democracy, the practice of education and the constitution of the nation-state" have always been interminably bound together. The imperative before us as citizens is to engage a process of unthinking our colonial roots and rethinking democracy. For teachers and students, this means that we must be willing to act as agents of transgression, posing critical questions and engaging dangerous discourse. Such is the basis of Red Pedagogy. (Grande, 2015)

Red Pedagogy is primarily a pedagogical project. In this context, pedagogy is understood as being inherently political, cultural, spiritual and intellectual. It is fundamentally rooted in the indigenous knowledge and praxis. It is particularly interested in knowledge that furthers understanding and analysis of the forces of colonization.

Critical theories of education have a major backing in the formation of Red Pedagogy. A red pedagogy searches for ways it can both deepen and be deepened by engagement with critical and revolutionary theories and praxis. It promotes an education for decolonization and within red pedagogy, the root metaphors of decolonization are articulated as equity, emancipation, sovereignty, and balance. In this sense, an education for decolonization makes no claim to political neutrality but rather engages a method of analysis and social inquiry that troubles the capitalist-imperialist aims of unfettered competition, accumulation and exploitation.

Red Pedagogy is a project that interrogates both democracy and indigenous sovereignty. In this context, sovereignty is broadly defined as a people's right to rebuild its demand to exist and present its gifts to the world...an adamant refusal to dissociate culture, identity and power from the land (Lyons, 2000)

In the views of Grande, Red Pedagogy actively cultivates praxis collective agency i.e. it aims build transcultural and transnational solidarization among indigenous people and others committed to reimagining a sovereign space free of imperialists, colonialists, and capitalist exploitation. It is grounded in hope; a hope that lives in contingency with the past—one that trusts the beliefs and understandings of our ancestors, the power of traditional knowledge and possibilities of new understandings.

Red pedagogy aims at adopting a revolutionary critical pedagogy which is made possible when children belonging to the marginalized section of the society are not only given educational opportunities but also the environment to preserve their culture. They are able to value and respect their culture and their teacher and peers are also able to respect the cultural differences.

The NCF (2005) states that "When children and teachers share and reflect on their individual and collective experiences without fear of judgment, it gives them opportunities to learn about others who may not be a part of their own social reality. This enables them to understand and relate to differences instead of fearing them."

Red Pedagogy comes out of that principle of critical pedagogy which encourages individuals to celebrate their socio-cultural differences and to learn from them.

Thus the adoption of critical pedagogy can help in changing the education set up of the society for the better. It can balance out the unequal power relations and make the "classroom environment democratic."

In the following paragraphs meaning and significance of democracy in education are highlighted.

Democratic Classroom Environment

Classroom is a mini Society with in itself. The features of the concern society get representation in a classroom situation. Multi-ethnicity of society: starting from gender, economic disparity, social inequality, caste, religion, regional differences and what not? In this context we can say that classroom is a large representation of the Society. Now if a Society claims to be a democratic then the school and classrooms should inculcate qualities of a democratic citizens; similar environment has to be provided in the classroom. To create democratic classroom we should consider the following:

A. *Classroom as a Society*: Every classroom is a true miniature of the society concerned and this has been experienced by many of us. The levels of diversity and differences, which we observe in society, do exist in the classroom. This should be taken as an advantage for the concept of a democratic classroom, where educators don't need to create a scenario to help students understand society, but can help them practicing democratic principles in the given conditions, which will surely help them to be responsible and sensitive citizens for society at large.
B. *Teacher as a Democratic Leader*: Here, the catch is that, no democratic model can get success, until it has leaders who not only believe in democracy but, also, practice it in the social and political arena. They are meant to encourage and promote democracy through their words and actions. In the same way, a teacher, in a democratic classroom model, needs to be a true leader and a strong believer of democratic principles. She/he needs to involve students in all the possible stages of decision making, as this would be the best approach of preparing citizens for a democratic society.
C. *School as a Democratic Government*: With the introduction of the right to education bill (2009), there is a provision to have a school managing committee for each government school. The composition of the managing committee is proposed in such a way that the community gets maximum participation and feels involved and empowered in the working of the school in its locality. In the same way, the concept of a true democratic school remains incomplete, until the student community is given representation in the decision making body at all levels of the working of the school. This would surely help the youth to learn and practice decision making at top level of the functioning of the school. In a way, this would be a forum for students to actively participate in legislative and executive bodies at the school level.

D. ***Students as Empowered Citizens***: with the three initiatives mentioned above, students are oriented and encouraged to behave like empowered citizens in a mini society i.e. school/ classroom level. This would be a great support to the cause of democracy in the modern era. The modern generation doesn't go by the theory of a lifestyle, but they want to have true role models around them. When these young students will be treated as empowered citizens, then there is a greater possibility of them taking up an active role of empowered citizens in the real world.

A democratic classroom is one in which students have equal opportunity to be heard and treated respectfully and fairly. Creating a democratic classroom environment means involving students, on a regular basis and in developmentally appropriate ways, in shared decision making (on various issues like curriculum, instruction, evaluation, discipline, time schedules, etc) that increases their responsibility to make the classroom a better place to learn.

Thus, the following three principles used as a basis for instructional decisions constitute democratic classroom practice (Parker, 1996; Ravitch and Thernstrom, 1992):

- Liberty and freedom
- Justice and fairness
- Equality and equal opportunity

The NCF (2005) highlights adopting democratic principles in a classroom environment by sticking to the value of equality and putting an end to any sort of discrimination on the basis of the socio-economic background of the learner.

The teacher is required to act as a role model for the promotion of a democratic environment and outlook and the teacher should not promote stereotypes.

In the NCF it is clearly stated,

> "A matter of serious concern is the persistence of stereotypes regarding children from marginalized groups, including SC and ST, who traditionally have not had access to schooling or learning. Some learners have been historically viewed as uneducable, less educable, slow to learn, and even scared of learning. There is similar stereotype regarding girls, which encourages the belief that they are not interested

in playing games, or in mathematics and science. Yet another set of stereotypes is applied to children with disabilities, perpetuating the notion that they cannot be taught along with other children. These perceptions are grounded in the notion that inferiority and inequality are inherent in gender, caste and physical and intellectual disability. There are a few success stories, but much larger are the numbers of learners who fail and thus internalize a sense of inadequacy. Realizing the constitutional values of equality is possible only if we prepare teachers to treat all children equally. We need to train teachers to help them cultivate an understanding of the cultural and socio-economic diversity that children bring with them to school."

Many of our schools now have large numbers of first generation school goers. Pedagogy must be reoriented when the child's home provides any direct support to formal schooling. First-generation school goers, for example, would be completely dependent on the school for inculcating reading and writing skills and fostering a taste for reading, and for familiarizing them with the language and culture of the school, especially when the home language is different from the language of school. Indeed they need all the assistance they can get.

Many such children are also vulnerable to conditions prevailing at home, which might make them prone to lack of punctuality, irregularity and inattentiveness in the classroom. Mobilizing inter sectorial support for freeing children from such constraints, and for designing a curriculum sensitive to these circumstances, therefore is essential.

The following are the experiences and views of various teachers and educators on democratic classrooms.

J'Anne D. Ellsworth (Professor and Teacher educator) talks about how she made her classroom a democrating one in her article – "The Democratic Classroom: Giving Students Power". She suggested –

- Making due dates of projects suggested by students
- Making attendance on student's wish
- Sharing syllabus formation with students
- Group discussion and learning
- Be friendly etc.

She says that above guidelines makes students anxious in beginning but slowly when they feel competent and empowered, they end to score well. According to her, structure, balance and respect are critical components in building the type of student-teacher relationship that facilitates a democratic learning environment.

A citizen teacher can provide an environment where students think independently and understand the characteristics of a democracy. Does your classroom align with a democratic theme?

Organizing a classroom around principles of democracy is not new to American education. The principles that provide a background for this type of organization are found in classical Greek thought and more recently in the American colonial period (Smith, 1984). Three principles are discussed in this article: liberty and freedom; justice and fairness; and equal opportunity (Parker, 1996; Ravitch and Thernstrom, 1992). Their use as a basis for instructional decisions constitutes democratic classroom practice.

Democratic education, however, was not without adherents to teaching a common knowledge core. Around the early 1990s, some curriculum theorists (Olive 2001; Tanner and Tanner, 1995) suggested that common core knowledge (e.g., mathematics, social studies, science) could be enhanced by a parallel pedagogy-the integration of democratic principles into classroom practices. Parker (1996;, 2001) posited that common core knowledge should be taught in schools; however, the pedagogical practices of self-direction in creativity applying knowledge have been suggested to enhance core knowledge retention.

Not all policy makers agree with the suggestion for pedagogical integration of democratic practices; rather, they argue that the three principles of democratic thought should be implemented as a "Stand alone' approach in which teaching about democracy is a separate core content area of the curriculum (Gutmann and Thompson, 1996). For example, Lickona and Skillen (1993) pointed out that character education (developing a moral stance) is an important function of public schools. Lickona (1997) suggested the following elements for a comprehensive model supportive of a democratic classroom curriculum: the role of the teacher as mentor, helping children develops moral discipline by use of ethical reflection and conflict resolution, and use of cooperative learning. Currently, the integration of democratic principles into a standards-based core curriculum appears to have prevailed. Teachers remain committed to teaching the state-mandated content standards; however, interest in modifications of instructional decisions to include democratic principles remains high (Pryor 2002).

Excerpts from 'Democratic Classroom' Workshop by Steve Bailey

In this workshop the focus is on how a teacher dealing with adolescents should understand the five areas of adult relationships with teen-agers that will encourage their positive growth namely –

1. Effective communication
2. Respect
3. Empowerment
4. Encouragement
5. Modeling

All these five areas are critical for the development of democratic classroom where adolescents are there. These components are given for Jewish school but hold true for every school.

A fundamental belief woven through this entire project is that it is critical for teachers and administrators who work with teen-agers to understand the basic nature of adolescent psychological developmental processes and the maturing nature of the adolescent. If the goal in Jewish education is to help shape the moral and ethical character of the student, interpersonal interactions between teacher and student become a critical necessary condition for teacher influence. To that end, let us discuss four characteristic areas of adolescent processes of particular relevance to educators:

- Self-Esteem
- Thinking Styles
- Defense Mechanisms
- Values

Adolescent issues are fairly universal and a teacher's knowledge of these basic developmental processes will help greatly in relating to the student effectively.

Encouraging Positive Adolescent Growth

There are five areas of adult relationships with teen-agers that will encourage positive growth: communication, respect, empowerment, support and modeling.

The challenge to educators is to minimize the negative expressions of adolescent dynamics and encourage the positive expressions.

In order to do this, it is necessary to learn about the ways adults, especially educators, can encourage the positive expressions of adolescent growth and minimize the negative.

Andrea Acker (2000) in her thesis on "Creating a democratic classroom, a gradual process" has used these components while teaching in classroom.

Many educators shy away from the democratic method of teaching out of fear. Many have tried and given up because the implementation is too difficult and time consuming. No one ever said that it is an easy task. It is a challenging venture into unknown territory for both teachers and students. But, in her essay, "To give my students wings," Katie Poduska asserts that the "choice to teach democratically is one in which I must dare to be different and to forge my own path" (Poduska 116). From the author's own experience, he tried to implement more student centered activities into his planning, and it was not a casual, immediate period of transition. In fact, he found it very arduous to implement democratic methods into his lesson plans. It is a process that takes a large amount of time and energy requiring innovative creativity.

Aziz H. Premji (2005) also focuses on a classroom to be democratic in his article 'Reforming our schools to chart social progress 'Fifty eight years after Independence, one question remains in my mind: why did we struggle for independence? For close to three centuries, British colonial rule was the norm for our countrymen. Even before the British, our nation had only known the rule of kings, monarchs and emperors. Having barely experienced any other form of governance, what then triggered the powerful Independence movement?

The answer lies in understanding that the independence movement was not a struggle against the British. Rather, it was a struggle for an idea of India—a democratic ideal that first existed in the minds of a few and then sparked an entire nation. Paraphrasing from our Constitution, this is the idea of a society where the spirit of brotherhood reigns among the people of India, transcending all diversity; a society that protects nature and has compassion for all living creatures; a society of humane citizens; a society that strives towards excellence in all spheres of individual and collective activity.

In this day and age, how many of us can truly relate to these word of Gandhiji:

> "I will give you a talisman. Whenever you are in doubt, or when the self becomes too much with you, apply the following test: Recall the face of the poorest and the weakest man whom you may have seen, and ask yourself if the step you contemplate is going to be of any use to him. Will he gain anything by it? Will it restore him to a control over his own life and destiny? In other words, will it lead to Swaraj for the hungry and spiritually starving millions?"

To begin with, it is clear that such a citizen cannot come forth in a classroom that is not democratic. In our schools, students are usually treated as beings who need to be didactically tutored, disciplined, and moulded. Students are "told" what to do, how to behave and what they must know. It seems that the first step is to make classrooms more open, friendly and democratic. A classroom, where the student is an active and equal participant in the teaching-learning process and is continuously formulating, questioning, thinking, experiencing, challenging, reconstructing—and thus learning.

The author's own experience is that a good teacher can impact a child deeply, simply because children learn by observing and trying to emulate adults. Therefore, the second requirement is to have teachers who are good role models. It is essential that our schools have teachers who are competent and committed; who are constantly learning; who are good listeners; who care about their students and about the world. And we have to help the teacher become this, and s/he has to try and become this.

The third step is to recognize that schools are important spaces for social learning. Here, the child learns how to relate to her classmate, to the person who keeps the school clean, to the authority of teachers, to the stray dog and to the tree in the playground. If the child learns to treat each being with love and equity, then the child will grow up learning to live in harmony with herself, and with respect and care for her world.

Let us end with the words of Swami Vivekananda:

> "Our duty is to encourage everyone in his struggle to live up to his own highest idea, and strive at the same time to make the ideal as near as possible to the Truth. Education is not the amount of information that is put into your brain and runs riot there, undigested all your

> life. We must have life-building, man-making, character-making, assimilation of ideas. If you have assimilated five ideas and made them your life and character, you have more education than any man who has got by heart a whole library."

With the adoption of Critical Pedagogy, a teacher can make the classroom environment democratic which will lead to the development and growth of not a selected few but all the students. Students will themselves be able to value the vital principles of a democracy and will help in strengthening and protecting it in all the areas of their life.

6

Evaluation and Assessment in Political Science

Meaning, Nature and Need of Evaluation

Evaluation is a process which helps in analyzing the performance of the student and the success of the teaching strategy employed by the teacher. It involves testing, measuring and judging the abilities of the students with reference to the expected or standard objectives. (Kumar, 2015) Evaluation helps in understanding the strengths and weaknesses of the students so that the students as well as the teachers can make changes in the teaching-learning processes and improve the learning outcomes.

Techniques of Evaluation in Social Science—Political Science

Evaluation can be carried out through several ways which can help in measuring the teaching learning outcomes. The teacher can make use of the following to evaluate the performance and the learning outcome of the students-

1. Oral tests and examinations
2. Witten tests and examinations which may include objective type questions, short answer type questions and long answer or essay type questions.
3. Practical tests and examination
4. Techniques and devices like observation, discussion, questionnaire, interview, checklist, rating scale etc.

The CBSE CCE Manual (2010), highlights the significance of evaluation as –

"Evaluation is goal directed, and educational outcomes are judged in terms of goal attainment. Every educational programme should aim for the all-round development of the personality of the child. Therefore, the learning experiences provided in the school should contribute toward the achievement of the desired goals.

The scope of evaluation in schools extends to almost all the areas of learners' personality development. It should include both scholastic and co-scholastic areas, i.e. it should be comprehensive in nature. This is in line with the goals of education."

It further states that Evaluation not only measures the progress and achievement of the learners but also, the effectiveness of the teaching materials and methods used for transaction. Hence, evaluation should be viewed as a component of curriculum with the twin purpose of effective delivery and further improvement in the teaching learning process. (CBSE CCE Manual, 2010)

The traditional system of evaluation was associated only with examination. In the NCF (2005), it is highlighted how "In the Indian education system, the term evaluation is associated with examination, stress and anxiety....We are concerned about the ill effects that examinations have on efforts to make learning and teaching meaningful and joyous for children. Currently, the board examinations negatively influence all testing and assessment throughout the school years, beginning with pre-school."

At the same time, a good evaluation and examination system can become an integral part of the learning process and benefit both the learners themselves and the educational system by giving credible feedback.

Education is concerned with preparing citizens for a meaningful and productive life, and evaluation should be a way of providing credible feedback on the extent to which we have been successful in imparting such an education

It is now realized by our curriculum framers that we need a curriculum whose creativity, innovativeness, and development of the whole being, the hallmark of a good education makes uniform tests that assess memorized facts and textbook -based learning obsolete.

We need to redefine and seek new parameters for and ways of evaluation and feedback. In addition to the learner's achievements in specific subject areas that lend themselves to testing easily, assessment would need to encompass attitudes to learning, interest, and the ability to learn independently.

The Board Exams for class 10 were made optional and the performance of the students was assessed not only on the basis of how well they fair in written examinations but also how they perform in various practical domains.

From the year 2017-18, the CCE model has been redefined and 10th boards is no more optional but is now being compulsory in all CBSE affiliated Schools. The assessment will be done by focusing on the Scholastic as well as the Co-Scholastic areas The performance of students in the scholastic areas will be assessed by their performance in 5 academic subjects which would include a periodic test, notebook submission (which includes notes prepared in the classroom as well as the assignments) and subject enrichment activities which are recorded internally by the respective subject teachers. The performance of the students in Co-Scholastic activities, for the holistic development of the student would be assessed by the students' performance in work education or pre-vocational education, art education, and health and physical education (CBSE, 2017)

Evaluation and Assessment

The word "assessment" comes from the Latin verb, "assidere" meaning, "to sit with". This word's origin implies that in assessment the teacher sits with the learner and assessment is something teachers do *with* and *for* students rather than *to* students (Green, 1998 as quoted in Stigler, 2010)

With assessment the teacher monitors the success of teaching-learning in achieving the intended learning objectives for the students. Assessment also helps in finding out how the students dealt with the learning material and the process of learning.

Teachers can assess students before instruction, during instruction and after instruction. Assessment before instruction is used to get an idea of what students already know or their previously attained knowledge. Assessment during instruction can be used to determine what students are learning so that the teacher can mold her/his teaching, if required." Assessment of students after instruction is used for two purposes: (1) to determine if there has been a change in knowledge (final exams can be used for "summative assessment"); and (2) to provide you with information to revise the class or program.

Evaluation involves a judgment by the teacher about whether the program or instruction has met its Intended Learning outcomes. It focuses on grades and may reflect classroom components other than course content and mastery level. These could include discussion, cooperation, attendance, and verbal ability. (T. Angelo, 1993)

Assessment on the other hand doesn't involve judgment; it focuses on learning, teaching and outcomes. It provides information for improving learning and teaching. Assessment is an interactive process between students and teachers that informs teachers how well their students are learning what they are teaching. The information is used by the teachers to make changes in the learning environment, and is shared with students to assist them in improving their learning and study habits. This information is learner-centered, course based, frequently anonymous, and not graded. (T. Angelo, 1993)

Assessment also helps the learners to get a feedback and become aware of their strengths and weaknesses. They are able to strive for the standards which have been set up for them

The CBSE CCE Manual states, "The overall goal of assessment is to improve student learning. It provides students, parents and teachers with valid information concerning student progress. Assessment involves the collection of evidence of student performance over a period of time to measure the level of learning and understanding. Evidence of learning could take the form of dialogue, journals, written work, portfolios and tests along with many other learning tasks." (CBSE, CCE Manual, 2010)

As per the NCF (2005), the purpose of assessment is necessarily to improve the teaching-learning process and materials, and to be able to review the objectives that have been identified for different school stages by gauging the extent to which the capabilities of learners have been developed.

Not only frequent examinations but routine activities and exercises can be employed effectively to assess learning. (NCF, 2005) Some of the features of good assessment tasks are that, it is based on the curriculum, students must know what is expected out of them, students must find the task to be worthwhile and relevant, and the task must be able to elicit optimal performance from students. (CBSE CCE Manual, 2010)

Assessments and examinations must be credible, and based on valid ways of gauging learning. Assessment needs to be valid in that valid it tests a relevant skill or ability and reliable so that the same result is achieved if the assessment is repeated. Credible assessment provides a report, or certifies the completion of a course of study, providing other schools and educational institutions, the community and prospective employers with information regarding the quality and extent of learning. (NCF, 2005)

A good assessment task or examination is one which is age appropriate and is based on the student's level of learning. The task's focus should not be to assess learner's ability to remember and recall textbook knowledge as, it would just encourage rote learning. Learners will not be able to think critically and hone their problem solving skills.

The NCF (2005), states that "the assessment should be carried out in a manner that it takes into account the subject knowledge of the learners. It must be able to gauge what learners have learnt, and their ability to use this knowledge for problem solving and application in the real world. In addition, they must also be able to test the processes of thinking to gauge if the learner has also learnt where to find information, how to use new information, and to analyse and evaluate the same."

Teachers are required to formulate such assessment tasks and tests which help the learners to hone their analytical and problem solving skills without increasing their stress and anxiety level. It should be such which can help the learner getting interested in what s/he learns and the learner is able to make use of their full potential.

Assessment can be grouped into two types:

1. Formative Assessment, and
2. Summative Assessment

Formative Assessment: It is something teachers do *with* and *for* students. Teachers involve students *with* them in the assessment thus, students and teachers are partners both sharing responsibility for learning. Formative assessment provides evidence for improving student learning. Indeed, to emphasize this function, it is often referred to as "assessment for learning." Lorna Earl (2003), also uses the phrase "assessment as learning, signaling the active role students play in the process.

It is a type of assessment which is continuous or ongoing integrated into instruction to collect evidence about how student learning is progressing towards learning goals. Formative assessment involves a variety of assessment methods and strategies there is no one way to conduct formative assessment.

Its aim is to get information about the learners' knowledge and performance and also to provide them with a feedback. Students get involved in self-assessment about how their learning is progressing so that they can be active agents in learning, working with teachers to diminish the gap between current levels of understanding and desired learning goals.

It is also helpful for the teachers as they get to know how effective the methods employed by them are and what has to be done to make them more effective. With formative assessment, the teacher becomes aware of the strengths and weaknesses of the learner and is able to assess her/him over a period of time and keep a note of the learning or performance graph.

It is used to make changes to alter the gap between current learning and desired goals

Some examples of formative assessments include asking students to:

- Draw a concept map in class to represent their understanding of a topic.
- Answering some questions or writing a paragraph in which they can explain what have they learnt and absorbed in a particular class.

Summative Assessment: It is an assessment which takes place at the end of the session or course. It helps determine whether a student has reached a certain level of competency "after completing a particular phase of education, whether it be a classroom unit, end of the year examination or 12 years of schooling (National Research Council, 2001, p.38 as quoted in Heritage, 2010). It is used to measure what students have learned, with little or no emphasis on using results to improve learning." (McMillan, 2007, p.7) Summative assessment usually involves taking an oral or written test of the learners and giving them the final scores. This type of assessment doesn't include feedback. The performance of the learner is rated on the basis of some standard grade or score. Example of summative assessment includes midterm examinations or final projects. Summative assessments are best thought of as retrospective. The vast majority of summative assessments in education are assessments of what the individual has learnt, know understand and can do. In contrast formative assessment can be thought of as being prospective (Wiliara, 2000, p.14 as quoted in Heritage, 2010)

Continuous and Comprehensive Evaluation (CCE)

CCE which is the continuous and comprehensive evaluation aims at evaluating and improving the student's performance by identifying her/his learning graph from time to time. This is the assessment which starts at the beginning of the academic year and continues till the end. It takes into account the evaluation of students that covers all aspects of their development.

"The 'continuous' aspect of CCE takes care for 'continual' and 'periodicity' of evaluation. Continual means, assessment of students in the beginning of instructions (placement evaluation) and assessment during the instructional process (formative evaluation) are done informally using multiple techniques of evaluation. Periodicity means assessment of performance done frequently at the end of unit/ term (summative) using criterion-referenced tests and employing multiple techniques of evaluation.

The 'comprehensive' component of CCE takes care of assessment of all round development of the child's personality. It includes assessment in scholastic as well as co-scholastic aspects of the pupils' growth. Scholastic aspects include curricular areas or subject specific areas, whereas co-scholastic aspects include co-curricular and personal social qualities, interests, attitudes, and values. Assessment in scholastic areas is done informally and formally using multiple techniques of evaluation continually and periodically. The diagnostic evaluation takes place at the end of unit/term test. The causes of poor performance in some units are diagnosed using diagnostic tests. These are purposefully re-mediated by giving intervention followed by retesting. Assessment in co-scholastic areas is done using multiple techniques on the basis of identified criteria, while assessment in social personal qualities is done using behavior indicators for various interests, values, attitudes, etc." (CBSE CCE Manual, 2010)

In India, CCE was adopted when the limitations of the traditional system of evaluation and assessment were realized. The traditional system of evaluation or assessment was such that it used to analyze the performance of the learner only on the basis of their performance in the examination. "In the Indian education system, the term evaluation is associated with examination, stress and anxiety."(NCF, 2005) So, complete dependence on examination for assessing the students' performance is an incomplete way of assessment.

Continuous and Comprehensive Evaluation at Different Stages

As the level of learning and understanding varies for learners of different stages so the assessment criterion for the learners performance should be such that it takes into account their level of physical and cognitive development.

Assessment should also be carried out in a way which is not stressful for the learners. They should not be burdened in any form and should be made to understand that it is for their own benefit. Written or oral tests should be introduced for assessment only when the child is able to deal with them. Other ways of assessment are observations of the development of the various domains of the learners, their performance in individual and group tasks and discussion with parents and peers.

The NCF (2005) has outlined how the assessment of students' performance should be done at different stages:

ECCE and Classes I and II of the Elementary Stage: At this stage, assessment must be completely based on qualitative judgments of children's activities in various domains and an assessment of the level of their health and physical development, based on observations through everyday participation and interactions. On no account should they be made to take any form of test, oral or written.

Class III to Class VIII of the Elementary Stage: At this stage a variety of methods may be used, including oral and written tests and observations. Children should understand that there performance is being assessed and they should not be made aware that it is a part of the teaching process and should not be taken as a fearful constant threat. At this stage grading or allocating marks along with qualitative judgments of achievement and areas requiring attention should be introduced. Children's own self-evaluation can also be a part of the report card from Class V onwards. Instead of lengthy examinations, there could be short tests from time to time, which are criterion based. Later, from class VII onwards term-wise examinations could be commenced. At this stage children are more psychologically ready to study large chunks of material and can spend a few hours in an examination room, working at answering questions without being restless. In this stage also the overall progress card of the learner must also indicate general observations on his/her health and nutrition, specific observations on the overall progress of the learner, and information and advice for the parents.

Class IX to class XII of the Secondary and Higher Secondary Stages: Assessment may be based more on tests, examinations and project reports for the knowledge-based areas of the curriculum, along with self-assessment. Other areas would be accessed through observation and also through self-evaluation.

The evaluation formulated for this stage could include much more analysis about the students, various skill/knowledge areas and percentiles, etc., This would assist them by pointing out the areas of study that they need to focus on, and also help them by providing a basis for further choices that they make regarding what to study thereafter. (NCF, 2005).

It is significant to be noted here that although CCE model of assessment is being adopted by various schools throughout the country but its success is yet to be achieved. Various lacunas in our education system such as in-appropriate student-teacher ratio, teachers orientation and low level of motivation and lack of proper planning and instruction makes the successful implementation of CCE impossible to achieve. The evaluation work is considered to be an extra burden for the teachers who are already loaded with both academic as well as administrative tasks. So for proper implementation of the CCE model proper planning is required.

Assessment Modes

There are various ways in which assessment can be carried out. Common mode of assessment is the one which is carried out by the teacher but there are other ways in which the individual can her/himself assess their performance and find out the lacunas if any. Assessment can also be carried out by the learner her/himself and by the co-learners or the peers who themselves were involved in the learning process. The sole purpose of all assessment modes continues to be getting aware of the performance for the improvement of the learning outcomes.

In the following paragraphs I have tried to explain the various modes in which assessment is carried out.

Self-Assessment

Assessment can be carried out with the involvement of the learner in the process. The learners' in consultation of their teacher establishes their own assessment criteria. In this process the learners are given the opportunity to reflect on and assess their learning experiences.

As per the NCF (2005), self-assessment experiences provide learners with self-regulatory capabilities essential for 'learning to learn'. Such information is also valuable feedback to the teacher, and can be used to modify the learning system as a whole.

Every classroom interaction with children requires their evaluation of their own work, and a discussion with them about what should be tested and the ways of finding out whether the competencies are being developed or not. Even very young children are able to give correct assessments of what they can or cannot do well. The role of teaching is to provide an opportunity to each child to learn to the best of his or her ability and provide learning experiences that develop cognitive qualities, physical well-being and athletic qualities, as also affective and aesthetic qualities.

Thus, self-assessment helps in increasing students' responsibility and autonomy and also makes them strive for a more advanced and deeper understanding of the subject matter, skills and processes. It upgrades the role and status of the student from passive learner to active leaner and involves students in critical thinking and reflection. Students are able to develop a better understanding of their own subjectivity and judgment.

Peer Assessment

As the name suggests, peer assessment refers to assessing the performance of students by their peers or classmates who were also involved in the learning process. Students individually assess each other's contribution using a predetermined list of criteria. Grading is based on a predetermined process, but most commonly it is an average of the marks awarded by members of the group. In peer assessment, the peers collectively decide a marking criterion with the help of their teacher this leads to preventing confusion about assignment outcomes and expectations. It also encourages student involvement and responsibility. They are able to reflect on their role and contribution to the process of the group work. The judgment skills of the students also gets honed.

Learners' Profile

A learner profile is basically a collection of information relating to individual learners who are engaged in the learning environment. In any course, it is always important for a teacher to know who her/his learners will be, where they come from, their previously attained knowledge and their expectations from the course.

Developing a learner profile helps teachers to better plan their teaching-learning process in a learner-centered way and to deliver the instruction in a manner that suits the individual preferences of the learner.

Learners' profile can be prepared by direct observation, personal surveys, collecting information from other subject teachers and parents.

Once learners' learning styles are known, it is easy to design instruction that accommodates their different learning needs. It is a fact that high achievers have different learning styles from low achievers. For instance, high achievers prefer to learn orally and visually while low achievers would prefer an extensive use of visuals because they find it difficult to remember information delivered orally through lectures and discussions.

Learner's Profile

School ....

(A) PERSONAL DETAIL

Paste your photo here

1) Name: ....
2) Class & section: ....
3) Roll no: ....
4) D.O.B./Age: ....
5) Father's Name: ....
6) Mother's Name: ....
7) Father's Occupation: ....
8) Mother's Occupation: ....
9) Address: ....
....
....
10) Phone Number: ....

(B) SELF AWARENESS

1) My Hobbies:
- ....
- ....
- ....

1) I want to become: ....
2) My role model is: ....

(C) SCHOLASTIC

Rating Scale

Always (1)   Mostly (2)   Sometimes (3)   Never (4)

✓ Class Participation

✓ Class Task

✓ Home Task

✓ Grasping Power

- ✓ Academics
- ✓ Discipline
- ✓ Linguistic Ability
- ✓ Project

(C) CO-SCHOLASTIC

Rating Scale

Very Good (1) Good (2) Average (3) Below Average (4)

THINKING SKILLS

- ✓ Creative
- ✓ Critical
- ✓ Decision Making
- ✓ General Awareness
- ✓ Reasoning Skills
- ✓ Questioning

SOCIAL SKILLS

- ✓ Discussion
- ✓ Attitude
- ✓ Participation for social cause
- ✓ Empathy/sensitive towards others

EMOTIONAL SKILLS

- ✓ Dealing With Stress
- ✓ Dealing With Controversial Issues
- ✓ Managing Emotion
- ✓ Problem Solving
- ✓ Expressive
- ✓ Attitude Towards School Property

(D) PERSONALITY

Rating Scale

Very Good (1) Good (2) Average (3) Below Average (4)

- ✓ Communication Skills
- ✓ Interaction With Batch mate
- ✓ Interaction With Teacher

- ✓ Helping Nature ☐
- ✓ Leadership Quality ☐
- ✓ Confidence ☐
- ✓ Punctuality ☐
- ✓ Regular ☐

TEACHER'S ASSESSMENT/SUMMITION

- ✓ A+ (90- 99%)
- ✓ A (80-89 %)
- ✓ B+ (70-79 %)
- ✓ B (60-69 %)
- ✓ C+ (50-59 %)
- ✓ C (40-49 %)
- ✓ D (33-39 %)
- ✓ E (Below 33 %)

◯

REMARKS (QUALITATIVE)

....
....
....
....
....

(Student's Signature) (Teacher's Signature)

Student's Feedback

Name: .... **R. No** ....

Instruction: To be filled up by Students, please tick (√) the appropriate option.

1. While teaching the topic, the teacher ask question to you.
   Always ☐ Mostly ☐ Sometimes ☐ Never ☐
2. Teacher asks for the feedback after the class.
   Always ☐ Mostly ☐ Sometimes ☐ Never ☐
3. Teacher calls you by your name
   Always ☐ Mostly ☐ Sometimes ☐ Never ☐

4. Whenever you ask question from the teacher, she/he answers to your question.

   Always ☐ Mostly ☐ Sometimes ☐ Never ☐

5. Language used by the teacher is easy to understand.

   Always ☐ Mostly ☐ Sometimes ☐ Never ☐

6. Activities done in the class make us busy and interested.

   Always ☐ Mostly ☐ Sometimes ☐ Never ☐

7. Do teacher give examples while teaching the chapter.

   Always ☐ Mostly ☐ Sometimes ☐ Never ☐

8. Teacher voice is clear and modulated.

   Always ☐ Mostly ☐ Sometimes ☐ Never ☐

9. Teacher gives updated information about the topic.

   Always ☐ Mostly ☐ Sometimes ☐ Never ☐

10. Teacher used ICT to teach you.

    Always ☐ Mostly ☐ Sometimes ☐ Never ☐

11. Teacher praise & encourage you for your effort and progress.

    Always ☐ Mostly ☐ Sometimes ☐ Never ☐

Open Text book Assessment (OTBA)

Open-book assessment is a mode of assessment which allows students to refer to their notes or textbooks while answering questions. Students can also be supplied with textual material in any form like an article, a case study, a diagram, a concept map, a picture or a cartoon, problem or situation based on the concepts taught to be students in previous classes. The focus is not on memorizing information, but on applying that information. Examinees are expected to not merely reproduce textbook material, but to interpret it in the context of specific questions and scenarios. Focus is laid on the thinking ability so it does not encourage rote learning. (Chopra, 2016)

The questions usually asked are the ones involving higher order thinking skills and some of which may be subjective, creative and open ended.

Conclusion

To sum up the discussion on the process of assessment, it is significant to reiterate the role of assessment which is to measure the progress that both learner and teacher have made towards achieving the aims that have been set and considering how this could be done better. Assessment should provide the learners with the opportunity for feedback so that they can work on themselves and bring about an improvement in their performance. It is also imperative that assessment should not bring about stress and anxiety as this would spoil the sole aim of assessment which is growth and betterment in learning outcomes.

With the help of assessment, the teacher and the learner should be able to judge not only the learning outcome but also the learning experience. The teacher is supposed to pay individual attention to each learner so as to assess their overall development.

Annexure I

2 Years B. Ed Syllabus,
Central Institute of Education, University of Delhi

Teaching of Political Science

Unit I Aims and Objectives of teaching Political Science

- Political Science in a democratic secular country; transition from 'civics' to political science
- Place of Political Science in secondary and senior secondary school curriculum; linkages between different stages; relations between Political Science and Social Science, Natural Science.
- Syllabi and Text books at different stages.

Unit II Issues and Challenges in Teaching-Learning of Political Science

- Pre-conceptions and misconceptions in Political Science
- Critical pedagogy in Political Science: Study of children's Idea of various concepts -Democracy, Government, Panchayat, Constitution, Rights, Duties etc. Its meanings, paradoxes' and challenges, limitations.
- Inclusive and Democratic Classroom for Political Science

Unit III Political Science Pedagogy

- Purpose, Approaches and Methods of teaching- learning of Political Science
- Inductive, Deductive, Interdisciplinary and Constructivist approaches in teaching-learning of Political Science
- Methods, Techniques and Resources:
  Traditional: lecture, question-answer, discussion, text book, storytelling,
  Modern: dialogue, problem solving, project, observation, debate, source,

excursion, dramatization, current events, empirical, comparative, community resource, mass media, case study, reflective enquiry and report writing.
- Theoretical basis and Development of Lesson Plan
- Teaching Learning Material: Need, objectives and preparation.

ICT in Political Science Classroom, Using PowerPoint, Excel, YouTube, Moodle, Blogs, etc. in the classroom. Use of Encyclopedia/Newspaper/Articles/Magazines/Journals in Social Science. Use of Maps/Charts/Graphs/Models/Pictures/Cartoons.

Unit IV Enriching Political Science

- Evolution and Development of Political Science Contemporary Trends in Political Science: Political Science in global context, Political- Social Dimension of Caste/Class/Religion/Gender with respect to current syllabi and textbooks.
- International Understanding and Peace and conflict resolution, Changing role of UN, Era of Coalition Government, Youth and Technology in Political affairs, Neo-liberalism and its implications, Role of Media and Judiciary in India
- Political Science Teacher: Personality, Outlook and Reflective Practitioner

Unit V Evaluation in Political Science

- Formative, Summative, Continuous and Comprehensive, Assessment at different stages.
- Assessment Modes: Self-assessment, Peer assessment, Learners' profile, Open textbook assessment.
- Preparation of a Question Paper and Analysis.

Suggested Practicum

a) Organization of Subject Society
b) Term papers on current issues: Citizenship, Gender issues in Indian Politics, Political Education, Political Science and scope of scientific enquiry, Exit polls etc.
c) Analysis of curriculum policies /documents and curriculum frameworks.
d) Critical appraisal of existing Political Science curriculum and text books at senior secondary school level
e) Development of Lesson Plan, Critical Lesson.
f) Visit to Parliament/Assembly in Session
g) Preparation of a Question Paper and Analysis
h) Action Research

Bibliography

Anderson, J.R. (2005). *Cognitive Psychology and its Implications (6th edition).* New York: Worth.

Arora, Pankaj (2006). Lesson Plan: A Means or an End, *MERI Journal of Education,* Number-I, April 2006, New Delhi.

Arora, Pankaj (2014). Exploring the Science of Society. *Journal of Indian Education.* NCERT, New Delhi.

Arora, Pankaj. (2015). *A Democratic Classroom.* New Delhi: Nirmal Publication.

Assessment and Evaluation. (n.d.). Retrieved july 2016, from Teaching and Learning Laboratory, MIT: http://tll.mit.edu/assessment/assessment-and-evaluation

Batra, P. (2010). *Social Science Learning in Schools: Perspective and Challenges.* New Delhi: Sage Publications India Pvt. Ltd.

Bains, J. (1971). The State of Political Science in India. *The Indian Journal of Political* Science, 393-444.

Bhushan, V. Sachdeva, D. R. (2012). *Fundamentals of Sociology.* Delhi: Pearson.

Bining, A.C. & Bining, D.H.(1932), *Teaching of Political Science in Secondary Schools.* Mumbai: Tata McGraw Hill Publishing Co. Ltd.

Bryce, J. (1909). The Relations of Political Science to History and to Practice: Presidential Address, Fifth Annual Meeting of the American Political Science Association . *The American Political Science Review* , 1-19.

CBSE. (2015). Senior school curriculum 2015-2016, Main Subjects Volume 1. Delhi: Academics & Training Wing, "Shiksha Sadan", 17 Rouse Avenue.

CBSE. (2010). Continuous and Comprehensive Evaluation Manual for Teachers Classes 9 and 10. Delhi: CBSE.

CBSE. (2017, January 31). Notification-Restoring of class 10 board examination with effect from the academic year 2017-18. Retrieved March 11, 2017, from CBSE: http://cbse.nic.in/newsite/attach/10th%20Board%20Exam%20English.pdf

Centre, E. (n.d.). Whys and Hows of Assessment. Retrieved July 2016, from Carnegie Mellon University: https://www.cmu.edu/teaching/assessment/basics/formative-summative.html

Chopra, R. (2016, January 11). HRD ministry urges state, central school boards to consider open-book tests at board level. *The Indian Express.*

Constructivism as a paradigm for teaching and learning. (2004). Retrieved 2016, from Concept to Classroom: http://www.thirteen.org/edonline/concept2class/ constructivism/index.html

Christudason, A. (1994). The Debate as a learning tool. Retrieved December 11, 2015, from Successful Learning: http://www.cdtl.nus.edu.sg/ success/sl11.htm

Datta, P. K. (1989). Political Science in India: An Inquiry into the Present State of the Discipline. *Indian Journal of Political Science*, 272-280.

Deepa Sapra, Gauri Srivastava, R.S. Pasricha, M.A. Hussain, R. Raizada, Saroj Pandey, Mily Roy, P.K Das Basabi Khan Banerjee. (2003) Self Instructional Package in Social Sciences for Upper Primary Teachers. New Delhi: NCERT.

Dubey, R. (2008-2009). Nagrik Shastra Ke Bachav Me- Ek Acadaemic Behas. Sanchetna , 70-78.

Edgar, B.W. & Stanely (1938), Teaching Social Studies in High School, Boston D.C.: Heath and company.

Farooq, U. (2014, July 31). Audio Visual Aids in Education: Definition, Types and Objectives. Retrieved November 22, 2015, from Study Lecture Notes: C:\Users\ABC\Desktop\Audio Visual Aids Intro, Definition, Advantages & Characteristics SLN.mht

Faravani, A. (n.d.). Gestalt Problem Solving. Retrieved July 2016, from scribd: file:///C:/Users/HP/Desktop/Gestalt%20Problem%20Solving.htm

Fernandes, L. (1990). Political Science in India- The Crux. *The Indian Journal of Political Science*, 15-21.

Gallanvan & Kottler, Ellen (2008), *Secrets to Success for Social Studies Teachers*. Thousand Oaks, CA: Crowin Press, Sage Publication.

Garforth, F. (1980). *Educative Democracy*. John Stuart Mill. New York: Oxford University Press.

George, A., M. & Madan, A. (2009). *Teaching Social Science in Schools*. New Delhi: Sage Publications India Pvt. Ltd.

Giroux, H. (1984). Ideology, Culture and the Process of Schooling. Philadelphia: Temple University Press.

Giroux, H. (2010) "Lessons From Paulo Freire", "https://en.wikipedia. org/wiki/Chronicle_of_Higher_Education" \o "Chronicle of Higher Education".

Giroux, H. (2009). Teacher education and democratic schooling. In A. Darder, M. P. Baltodano, and R. D. Torres (Eds.), *The critical pedagogy reader*, second edition. (pp. 438-459). New York: Routledge. As quoted in Wylie, S. (2014). The Challenge of Critical Pedagogy as a Social Studies Teacher Educator. PhD Thesis

Golsmith, A. H. (2012). Interdisciplinary Approaches to Teaching. Retrieved january 2, 2016, from Pedagogy in Action the SERC Portal of Education: http://serc.carleton.edu/sp/library/interdisciplinary/index.html

Heritage, M. (2010). *Formative Assessment- Making it happen in the classroom*. California: SAGE Limited.

Hopper, J. (n.d.). 5 New Approaches to Teaching and Learning. Retrieved August 16, 2016, from Scribd: https://www.scribd.com/document/232288317/5-New-Approaches-to-Teaching-and-Learning

Introduction about SCERT. (2014, March 24). Retrieved January 13, 2017, from delhi.gov.in:http://delhi.gov.in/wps/wcm/connect/doit_scert/Scert+Delhi/Home/ About+SCERT/Introduction

J.Patrick, J. (2006). *Understanding Democracy.* Madison Avenue, New york: Oxford University Press.

Kochhar, S.K. (1983), *Methods and Techniques for Teaching History.* New Delhi: Sterling Publishers Pvt. Ltd

Kirkpatrick, Ecron, (1997). *Foundation of Political Science: Research, Methods and Scope*, New York: The Free Press.

Krishna Kumar. (2004) *What is Worth Teaching.* Delhi: Orient Blackswan.

Lexington,M.D.(2016).JohnDewey-HowWeThink:WhatisThought.Retrieved 2016, from A John Dewey Source Page: file:///C:/Users/HP/Desktop/John%20Dewey%20%20How%20We%20Think%20%20Chapter%201%20%20What%20is%20thought.htm

Maria Evangelou, K. S. (2009, November). Early Years Learning and Development. Retrieved from (https://www.gov.uk/government/uploads/system/uploads/ attachment data/file/222003/DCSF -RR176.pdf)

M.H Siddiqui. (1993). *Teaching of Economics.* Delhi: APH Publishing Corporation.

Narang, R. H. (1992). Social Justice and Political Education through Non-Formal Education. *Springer*, 542-546.Retrieved December 9, 2014, from http://www.jstor.org/ stable/3444692

NCF. (1988). New Delhi: NCERT.

NCF. (2000). New Delhi: NCERT.

NCF. (2005). New Delhi: NCERT.

NCTE. (2009). NCTE Draft for Discussion. New Delhi: NCTE.

O.P. Dhiman (2008). *Understanding Education: An Overview.* Delhi: Kalpaz Publications.

O.P. Gauba (2000). *An Introduction To Political Theory* (4 Edition). Macmillan India Limited.

Panel Discussion: A Manual For Practising Teachers. (2008). Jammu, India: MIER College of Education.

Prakash, O. (2008). NCF 2005 ke sandarbh me madhyamik star par (samajik vigyan ke antergrat) 'nagrik shastra' upvishya ki 'rajneetisastra' me badalne ki sarthakta ka addhyan. New Delhi: M.ed Dissertation.

Pravah. (2009) *Nurturing Youth: Active Citizenship in India: report on a stakeholder Consultation.* New Delhi.

Problem Solving. (2009, April). Retrieved July 2006, from Cognitive Psychology: file:///C:/Users/HP/Desktop/Problem%20Solving%20-%20Cognitive%20Psychology.

R.P Pathak. (2012). *Teaching of Social Studies.* Delhi: Pearson Education.

Richard Mayer and Merlin Wittrock. 23 December 2009. http://www.education.com/reference/article/problem-solving, 11 January 2016

The Reflective Teaching Model. (2016). Eastern Mennonite University: http://www.emu.edu/education/model/, 16 July 2016

Sandeep Kumar. (2015). *Child development and Pedagogy*. Delhi: Pearson.

Sandy Grande (2015). Red Pedagogy: Native American Social and Political Thought. North America: Rowman and Littlefield.

Self and peer assessment – advantages and disadvantages. (n.d.). Retrieved 2016, from The University of Sydney: https://sydney.edu.au/education_social_work/ groupwork/docs/SelfPeerAssessment.pdf

Shah, G. (2001). Political Science in India: A Discipline and Intellectual Pursuit. *The Indian Journal of Political Science*, 11-23.

Shwartz, M. (2011). learning and teaching office. Retrieved 2016, from Ryerson University: "http://www.ryerson.ca/content/dam/lt/resources/handouts/CaseMethod GroupWork.pdf"

Stavros Ioannides, K. N. (2007). *Economics and the Social Sciences: Boundaries, Interaction and Integration*. Edward Elgar Publishing.

T. Angelo, T. a. (1993). Classroom Assessment Techniques. In *Classroom assessment techniques a handbook for College teachers* (p. 427). San Fransisco: Jossey-Bass A Wiley Imprint.

Teacher Education. (2016). Retrieved august 2016, from MHRD: file:///C:/Users/HP/Desktop/Teacher%20Education%20_%20Government%20of%20India,%20Ministry%20of%20Human%20Resource%20Development.htm

Thomas. R. Dye. (2016). *Politics in America* 10th Edition. Cram 101. Retrieved july 2016, from "http://www.allreadable.com/75beFjUa

Tilak, L. (n.d.). *Political Education by Lokmanya Tilak.* Retrieved from http://www.ncte-india.org/pub/tilak/4.7.htm)

Unit Planning. (2011). Retrieved March 8, 2016, from Teaching as Leadership: http://teachingasleadership.org/sites/default/files/RelatedReadings/IPD_Ch4_2011.pdf

Wagner, P. (1999). The Twentieth Century - the Century of the Social Sciences? World Social Science Report.

Washington, C. (2011). Inductive Deductive Methods. Retrieved july 2016, from Scribd: https://www.scribd.com/doc/306828407/Inductive-Deductive-Methods

Willingham, D.T. (2007). *Cognition: The thinking animal (3rd edition)*. New Jersey: Pearson.

Wojcik, M. (2009). *Political Education.* Retrieved from Youth4Media: http://rcie.home.pl/y4m/wp/?page_id=57

Wringe, C.(1984). *Democracy, Schooling and Political Education*. Sydney, Australia: George Allen and Unwin Ltd.

Wylie, S. (2014). The Challenge of Critical Pedagogy as a Social Studies Teacher Educator. PhD Thesis.

Zevin, J., (2000), *Social Studies for the Twenty First Century*. London: Lawrence Erilbaum Associates Publishers.